unwound

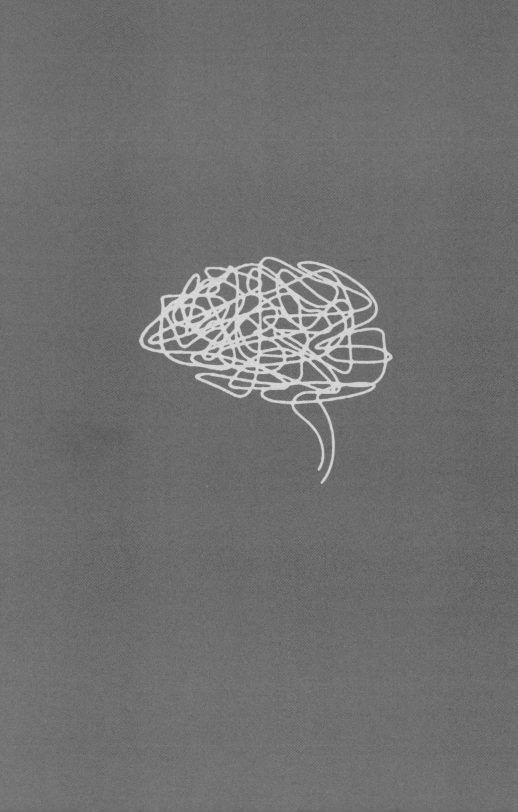

unwound

REAL-TIME
REFLECTIONS
FROM
A $TUMBLING
ENTREPRENEUR

ethan senturia

blackbird
VENTURES

La Jolla, California

Copyright © 2018 Blackbird Ventures

978-0-9831704-7-1 (hardcover)

978-0-9831704-8-8 (paperback)

978-0-9831704-9-5 (ebook)

2223 Avenida de la Playa, Suite 206
La Jolla, CA 92037

www.ethansenturia.com

PUBLISHING CONSULTING AND PRODUCT DEVELOPMENT:
BookStudio, LLC
www.bookstudiobooks.com

BOOK DESIGN:
Charles McStravick

Library of Congress Control Number: 2017956147

PRINTED IN THE UNITED STATES OF AMERICA

contents

'Tis a lesson you should heed,
Try, try again;
If at first you don't succeed,
Try, try again;
Then your courage should appear,
For if you will persevere,
You will conquer, never fear;
Try, try again.

Once or twice, though you should fail,
Try, try again;
If you would at last prevail,
Try, try again;
If we strive, 'tis no disgrace
Though we do not win the race;
What should you do in the case?
Try, try again.

If you find your task is hard,
Try, try again;
Time will bring you your reward,
Try, try again;
All that other folks can do,
Why, with patience, should not you?
Only keep this rule in view:
Try, try again.

— T.H. PALMER, *The Teacher's Manual*

the
opening bell

MY GREATEST SUCCESS was a spectacular failure. After nearly five years of being overworked and underpaid in pursuit of the American Dream, I was alone and unemployed, tears running down my face, overwhelmed by the feeling that I'd just thrown my life away. The only proof that time had actually passed were the casualties left along the way: thirty million dollars of investor capital, sixty employees, tens of vendors, and any modicum of self-confidence I'd had to begin with. After laying off my team, breaking the news to the investors, and closing our doors, it was now a certainty, what days before had only been a possibility—I was a failed CEO.

That this happened was painful, but not unique. The statistics on startups show rather clearly that venturing to build a scalable, high-growth, disruptive business is, at best, like trying to hit a 100-mile-per-hour fastball and, at worst, like walking on water— that is to say, impossible. Even the most celebrated entrepreneurs have experienced great failures, and often their successes are a direct byproduct of their prior shortcomings. In fact, the prevailing gospel in startup culture is that failure is a rite of passage on the road to becoming a "real" entrepreneur. Like a supermodel airbrushed free of blemishes, an entrepreneur without warts is eyed skeptically as not quite human.

But as much as Silicon Valley accepts failure—and even rewards it—the conceptual embrace of striking out offers scant consolation to the individual who swings and misses. Neither stories nor statistics of failed entrepreneurs getting second chances, making valiant comebacks, or succeeding at higher rates[1] are likely to convince you that you will be one of them. Through a lens of subsequent success, it's easy to retrospect on failure as a blessing. But without the benefit of hindsight—in your precise moment of collapse—seeing it as a curse is more likely.

At some point during the wind-down, the CEO of a similarly sized competitor asked if she could speak with me to learn how she might avoid the same fate. Before diving into substantive dialogue, she expressed wonderment that I'd mustered enough courage to have a conversation after what transpired at Dealstruck. As she quickly went through the unpleasant exercise of envisioning herself in my shoes she conceded, "I can't imagine what it feels like to be you right now. I think if it were me, I'd probably be on my couch drunk for the next two years."

My response: "I don't think that's a great coping mechanism."

She wasn't the first person I'd spoken to who imagined they would resort to substance abuse when faced with failure or who had already done so when failure arrived. Though numbing ourselves to reality is not a particularly constructive approach for overcoming our shortcomings, it seems to be a common tactic adopted by entrepreneurs or startup executives confronting professional setbacks. Perhaps our unpreparedness to handle failure is nothing more than a failure of imagination.

---

1   Research published in 2014 by Stanford Graduate School of Business (GSB) Professor Kathryn Shaw reveals that multiple-time entrepreneurs, even outside of the tech industry, have progressively higher rates of success as measured by business longevity. Her conclusion, captured neatly in the title of a Stanford GSB Insights article summarizing her research, is that "Entrepreneurship Requires Practice, Practice, Practice."

If you had asked me at the outset of my adventure to paint a picture of success, I could have done so in fine detail. But had you asked me to do the opposite, I would have drawn a blank. We don't like thinking about failure—its common causes, its honest consequences, its psychological challenges—in part because we tend to believe the act of doing so will make it more likely. Ask newlyweds to consider the finer points of divorce and you'll likely hear uncomfortable chuckles followed by, "No, thanks, that won't happen to us." We love to contemplate the futures we desire, but hate to contemplate those futures we don't. What we miss in our unwillingness to explore these less-than-desirous outcomes is that defining the negative can be the most powerful force for realizing the positive.

The Roman philosopher Seneca is often credited with saying, "Luck is what happens when preparation meets opportunity."[2]

In the startup world, nary a soul will share a story of success in which luck doesn't play a central role. If luck is a necessary ingredient for success, and if preparation is a necessary ingredient for luck, then being conscious of all the paths your journey may follow—even the unsavory ones—is a critical step in preparing to succeed. It's a step I wish I had taken.

I'm certainly not the first entrepreneur to experience failure, nor am I the first to write about it. However, I have found most stories of failure tucked deep within larger tales of startup grandeur, entrepreneurial achievement, or professional redemption. While those accounts are inspiring and informative—I've consumed more than my fair share—they are reflections on failure by someone who has the comforting knowledge that success lies on its other side. The question that interested me as I grappled with my own defeat was not whether failure would fit neatly into the arc of a coherent narrative

---

[2]   There is some controversy around this quote's exact source and phrasing. It is believed to be a modern adaptation of a reference by Seneca in *On Benefits*, vii, to a quotation from Demetrius the Cynic, "The best wrestler is not he who has learned thoroughly all the tricks and twists of the art, which are seldom met with in actual wrestling, but he who has well and carefully trained himself in one or two of them, and watches keenly for an opportunity of practising them."

told looking back from my future; it was whether I could interpret failure as a positive situation while still in its midst.

This book is my effort to do that.

I'm fairly certain that staring deep into the heart of startup failure—wrestling with its psychology, untangling its twisted web, and confronting its unsavory truths—is a more effective prescription than staring deep into the bottom of a bottle. Plus, I can't hold my liquor.

Self-medication aside, on my last day at Dealstruck—when the furniture, the employees, and all other signs of life were gone—I walked to my car wondering, *If a tree falls in the forest and no one hears it, did it make a sound?*

That I was asking myself this question was not only disconcerting, but was evidence of the ease with which our minds naturally gravitate away from pain and toward pleasure. After spending five years consumed by Dealstruck my every waking moment (and some of my sleeping moments, too), I more than anyone should have been certain of its existence—but I wasn't. Were there really people working here? Did we really have over one thousand paying customers? Had I really built a company?

It sounds crazy, but the entire experience felt like a mirage.

I needed a way to assure myself that Dealstruck was real; that I had, in fact, created something from nothing, and that its lessons would not vanish quietly, but speak loudly to me forever.

This book is my effort to do that, too.

The creation of a tangible artifact to memorialize and learn from this chapter of my life was the most pleasant part of a rather unpleasant entrepreneurial endeavor. Though these words were written primarily as a cheap form of self-help and self-enlightenment, I figured the ease with which they could be shared made the prospect of them proving useful to a small number of entrepreneurs in some small way worth the effort, expense, and risk of publishing.

Among the greatest cathartic benefits of reliving my experience through written word was the opportunity to offer a recount free from the interruption, disagreement, or criticism of the story's many supporting actors. As a result, what follows is but one version of the Dealstruck saga. For my own benefit, I aspired to accuracy, to objectivity, and to intellectual honesty, but I'm quite certain I've come short of perfection. I'd be unsurprised to learn that others who have been touched by Dealstruck might offer an alternative perspective on what happened, why it happened, and who was responsible for it. They might focus on things I've wholly omitted, just as they might extract different insights from the stories or events I've chosen to include.

The simple fact that multiple perceptions of a single occurrence coexist does not necessarily invalidate any of them. Though I've tried to consider how an investor, vendor, employee, or partner might perceive the events I've retold, I'm limited by the fact that I've only seen them firsthand through one set of eyes. My time at Dealstruck was as a founder, a CEO, an entrepreneur, and I'm therefore most concerned with how things look from that vantage point. Though I'm confident in what I saw, I'm sure that others observing the same thing at the same time saw something entirely different. Undoubtedly, the truth lies somewhere in between.

Years from now, when the feelings have subsided and the details have faded from memory, I know it will be all too easy to reflect on Dealstruck as nothing more than some "crazy thing I did in my twenties." When I use the second person—"you" and "your"—I'm addressing a future self; I talk to "you" because I know tomorrow that could be me. Though it may sound like it, my intent in electing this voice is not to patronize or condescend, nor to project a righteousness I surely haven't earned. As soon as I finish writing, I'm no less a reader than you are, and I wrote my own story as I'd want it to be retold.

In reading my story, I hope you experience as much insight, emotion, and entertainment as I did in living it. Whether you love it or hate it, agree with me or disagree with me, feel frustrated and angry or empowered and understood, my wish is that our brief time together makes your step a little lighter, your mind a little quieter, your seas a little calmer, and your resolve a little sturdier in whatever grand adventure you undertake next.

CHAPTER 2

from womb
to wall street

MY FATHER IS A SUCCESSFUL serial entrepreneur. This means that for every one of his good outcomes he had many more bad ones, but managed to keep the magnitude of his infrequent wins greater than that of his more frequent losses. While the volatility of his professional life wreaked havoc on his marriage to my mother, resulting in his only devastating loss—"she sold too early" he would say—it made my childhood quite exciting. The only thing my father liked more than building startups was talking about them and, as a former Hollywood screenwriter, he could turn even the most mundane business tale into an action thriller.

He dubbed his little bits of startup knowledge his "rules" and, as a young child trying to relate to a single father maniacally focused on startup success, these "rules" became the pathway of our connection to each other ("return every phone call"—Rule #1—was a more common dinnertime directive than "eat your vegetables"). When I was seven, my mom and he divorced and the courts granted joint custody, so my sister and I were left with little choice but to spend lots of time in his office. Though I wasn't yet interested in the inner-workings of his business ventures, I had no trouble keeping myself occupied with the Ping-Pong tables and video game consoles in constant demand by his twenty-something-year-old geniuses during the "workday" (apparently the real magic happened at night). But beyond fun and games, being in the office provided me with important proof that my dad's "rules" had a basis in reality; he wasn't preaching something he never practiced—an all-too-common phenomenon in the startup racket where some who only *talk* about entrepreneurship confuse that with entrepreneurship itself.

So, I became a youthful Entrepreneur-in-Residence,[3] learning to negotiate (read: expanding my four-letter vocabulary), reviewing legal documents (read: finding out how they're trying to screw you), observing strategy sessions (read: figuring out how to get out of this mess), and building company culture (read: consuming pizza and beer). For the kids of many entrepreneurial parents, this sort of relationship—one in which work pervades, or even defines, an intimately personal bond—is the kind that results in lifelong therapy trying to cope with why "daddy wasn't there." For me, it was a window into a world of challenge, purpose, and excitement that most "normal people" never obtained from their work. What my dad and his devoted followers were doing seemed special and, by association, made me feel special, too.

Thus, at age thirteen, I decided I wanted to be in business. At that time, "business" was synonymous with whatever it was my dad was doing. I didn't realize that startups were a sideshow in a much grander circus—the knife-juggler playing to a small crowd, while the elephants and acrobats commanded center stage. I figured that every businessperson worked in a highly creative, risk-tolerant workplace with lots of energy, little hierarchy, and no bad ideas. I was so interested in business (or in pleasing my father) that I even

---

3   An Entrepreneur-in-Residence (EIR) is a position often awarded by venture capital firms to successful executives who are in between roles and who the venture investor would like to back on their next startup. The VC usually provides some compensation, office space, and administrative resources to EIRs so they have a comfortable perch to rest upon while they find the next big thing.

started a few entrepreneurial hustles myself—a lemonade stand, an eBay store, a sports book for my middle-school classmates.

None of these were wildly lucrative, but they laid the groundwork for my first real business victory—being accepted to the Wharton School of Business. I'm still not sure why I wanted to attend Wharton so badly. It probably had to do with my dad's regular lament that if he had started out with proper business training he would have been many times more successful (read: rich). Whether I was pursuing my true calling or merely living for my dad the life he wished he'd had, I was off to Wharton.

It took less than one week for me to realize that my conception of business was a bit different from most of my Wharton class-mates and almost the entire Wharton curriculum. I simply needed to open the first page of the *Daily Pennsylvanian* before my first semester even started, to see recruitment ads from Goldman Sachs, McKinsey, and every other big-name investment bank, consulting firm, and hedge fund. To be honest, I didn't know who most of those companies were, but the people around me sure did and they wanted to be part of them badly ("I would *die* to work at [insert firm name here]"). It was a rare day when I saw more Penn t-shirts tromping around Huntsman Hall than I did corporate logos. Who you wore represented who you knew, how smart you were, and how rich you would become—or at least, where you'd picked up a few slices of free pizza the night before.

With every passing moment at Wharton, the image of business conjured up in my childhood faded. Soon, I, too, was donning cor-porate logos and salivating at the prospect of a gold-plated job offer in the high-flying world of finance so that I could brag to my friends about starting salaries, annual bonuses, and upward mobility. These companies were *important*—after all, they were making headlines in the *Wall Street Journal*—and, my affiliation with one of them would make me important, too.

To my surprise, my father seemed to get off on the fact that I was going to be on Wall Street—that I would have a fancy job at a big firm, that I would be on the path to Managing Director, that his friends would recognize my company, that I might "dwarf him" in terms of wealth. For a guy who spent his whole life without a career progression, without a boss, without a corporate structure, whose specialty was creating something from nothing, and who now had Wall Street working *for him*, I suspected he'd be sad to see his son veer from his entrepreneurial footsteps. But I couldn't have been more wrong.

The romantic journey I had envisioned his professional life to be was, in reality, an extremely painful one. In his words, he was a total failure until his forties, at which point he was likely unemployable and certainly unmanageable. He became an entrepreneur because he had to. He wasn't good enough for his parents or his wife's parents, and, eventually, even for his wife. His investors and employees were either satisfied or upset, but never happy. And, he was always on the verge of being a failure or being fired. Even success, when it came, was more of a relief than a reason to rejoice. Who would want this life for his children?

So, he celebrated my leap from Wharton to Wall Street because it was *safe* and *certain*. If I woke up, wore a suit, and didn't throw up, I would always have a job. Maybe it wouldn't be fun, maybe it wouldn't be exciting, but it would be there. And, after "waging war" for his entire adult life, stability appealed to him (remember, I'm living the life he wanted).

The only problem is that two weeks after I started my Wall Street career it basically ended. In a last-ditch effort to convince myself I was not a total sellout, I chose to work at Lehman Brothers instead of Goldman Sachs (first-world problem, I know). After a brief period of mandatory training, I joined the High Yield Credit Research team full-time on September 2, 2008. On September 15th I was part of the largest corporate bankruptcy in American history. Exciting, yes. Safe and certain, no.

While I didn't lose my job—at $60k per year in New York City, I could have been replacing urinal cakes and still been a bargain— many of the people around me did. They cried. I didn't. They had a mortgage. I didn't. They lost their life savings. I didn't. Those who were "lucky" enough to stay on with Barclays—Lehman's buyer—didn't seem to feel that way. They lamented losing their stature (even at Barclays, they referred to themselves as "former Lehman"); they lamented losing their bonus (having a job when 35 percent of the industry was terminated wasn't enough); and they lamented losing their innocence (yes, they still expected life to be "fair").

Those who lost their jobs watched in terror as the financial services industry crumbled around them, forcing them to recognize that the same specialization that was once the primary cause of their job security was now the precise cause of their insecurity. "So, what does a bond trader do now?" People who poured their entire professional lives into doing one thing really well with the chief aim of assuring themselves regular employment and predictable income realized that in doing so they had violated one of the first rules of their own industry—diversification.

From my perspective, I saw two groups of people: the employed who wished they were employed elsewhere and the unemployed who didn't think they could get employed anywhere. I had no particular interest in my future self being part of either group, so I left. If you couldn't rely on a 158-year-old, multi-billion-dollar institution for job security, and you couldn't rely on skills honed finely over a professional lifetime, I figured partaking in either was a fool's errand.

For the eleven months I survived on Wall Street I had made it an afternoon ritual to take a short walk around the block, during which time I would call my mother to vent just enough pent-up frustration to make it through one more day. Our conversations always followed the same sequence—small talk at the start, complaining in the middle, and consolation at the end. By the time I had completed my loop and I found myself staring through a set of revolving doors I dreaded reentering, I would offer one last parting threat: "I might quit tomorrow."

Then one day, tomorrow finally came. That afternoon, I detoured from my usual route, instead taking a stroll into my bosses' office.

When I told them, "It's not you, it's me," they agreed. Apparently, my attempts to repress discontent while manning the desk were thinly veiled and, as a result, my resignation triggered as little surprise as it did sadness. Within minutes, my superiors had rushed back to the trading floor and I was packing my bag in advance of final goodbyes.

Given my brief tenure and junior position, I'm pretty sure I'd never registered as a blip on the radar of at least half the people to whom I bid farewell. However, of those with whom I had built some rapport—mostly the younger traders—I received an unexpected parting message: "Congratulations."

Leaving a highly coveted job for which I'd spent four years (and a few hundred-thousand of my parents' dollars) preparing for hardly seemed praiseworthy, but I guess I wasn't alone in my disillusion. That same night, when I crashed the tail-end of a company-sponsored first-year mixer, my peers greeted me with similar applause. I was confused—wasn't I the weak one? I had cracked, I couldn't cut it. The grand irony of that moment was that, as I stared at my former colleagues, envious and reverent of their discipline and willpower for staying, they stared back at me with an equal degree of envy and reverence for leaving.

A few months after I booked my last trade, I received an email update from my closest coworker, who was two years my senior. He wrote:

> *As for me, work is still fundamentally unsatisfying . . .*
> *I hate getting up at 5am and spending my days doing something*
> *I couldn't care less about, and dudes like you who manage to*
> *break the ties and go pursue interesting new things continue to*
> *serve as an inspiration.*

Ten years later, this person is still a Wall Street trader.

It's possible his career choice is the result of an evolved set of preferences. But it's also possible that it's the result of an ongoing wait for permission.

Whenever we make hard decisions, we want to know we're not alone. And, in our culture, there is no harder decision than to actively choose the life you *want* to have, rather than to passively accept the life you *should* have. When we first become aware of our own internal truths—the things we know serve us best—we often look outside ourselves for the "green light," convinced the only thing standing between us and action is an approving nod from the outside world. But this conclusion is false. For three hundred days, I'd cautioned my mom that I was on the verge of quitting, and for three hundred days she told me she would support me if I did. She could not have given me a more explicit license to leave, yet I stayed.

It turns out that to live the life you want, the hardest permission to obtain is the only permission you need—your own.

Nothing is more liberating than acting with your heart, not your head. As I walked off the trading floor, through the glass double-doors, and onto the elevator, I had—by all objective measures—made a mistake. I had no job, no plan, no income, and, at twenty-three years old, no particular skills of any merit. But I had never felt better.

employee
number one

.

MY PARENTS SAID THEY SUPPORTED ME quitting my job, moving home, and taking some time to figure things out, but I'm not sure I believed them. Nevertheless, I took them at their word and floated around for a while looking for something that intrigued me. I landed a couple of consulting gigs with startups: one for my father (nepotism at its finest) and one for an online textbook marketplace that, in spite of itself, wound up successful—proof that good luck can override even the most severe dysfunction. These were not glamorous jobs, nor did they have any particular value toward a "career path," but it felt good to be in a small startup environment where I wouldn't be scolded for a five o'clock shadow, an off-center necktie, or for simply being young.

The work wasn't particularly interesting, but I was deep into a period of self-loathing for having the arrogance to choose quality of life over professional achievement. Given that I had a long history of clinical depression, I was relatively comfortable wallowing in a pool of my own despair, so I didn't put much effort into finding a "real" job.

Fortunately, a job found me. In the fall of 2009, I received a phone call from a pair of former Wharton classmates two years my senior—Jesse Pujji and Nick Shah. During their waning days at Wharton, Jesse and Nick had recruited me to lead their custom shirt-printing business that took advantage of the wildly inelastic market resulting from Greek Life meeting Daddy's Amex. However, like most Wharton-ites, when adulthood came calling, Jesse and Nick forewent entrepreneurship in favor of more traditional jobs at Morgan Stanley and Goldman Sachs. After stockpiling some savings from the heady pre-crisis years, their entrepreneurial streak ultimately won out, prompting them to trade in their three-piece suits for 3-series BMWs and head to the West Coast to start a company.

Jesse's parents had relocated from St. Louis to San Diego a few years prior and, like any good entrepreneur, these guys were keeping overhead low by bumming a free room at Chez Pujji—a quaint McMansion in America's richest suburb. In the spirit of pattern recognition (the supposed "secret sauce" of venture investing), Jesse and Nick saw an opportunity for The Shirt Guyz to succeed all over again and took advantage of my entrepreneurial zeal (a.k.a. unemployment) to lure me in as the first employee in a scheme which, to that point, consisted solely of one thousand square feet of office space and a few cases of Red Bull.

Things started out well enough at Ampush (an amalgam of the founders' last initials). The first few months more closely resembled a book club than a business endeavor. Each day, we'd amble in mid-morning without any real sense of urgency, grab a How-To manual, and take one good hit from it before passing it left and moving to the next subject. Over lunch we'd share insights from our reading—hoping our meals wouldn't be the only things we'd digest—before retreating to the office to repeat the exercise until an unnecessarily late hour to at least act the part of an overwhelmed, stressed out, endlessly busy startup crew.

While you may not be able to learn entrepreneurship from a book—which could render useless this very one you are holding—you certainly can learn digital marketing.

The business we undertook was a simple one known as lead generation, the modern-day version of panning for gold. If the Internet is a giant river adrift with pollutants, debris, and all variety of stone, silt, and sediment, the lead generator's job is to bring up those nuggets that might be worth something. But that's where we stop. Rather than examine our own finds, we—in exchange for a fee—part with our would-be treasures, leaving the buyer with the more nuanced task of ascertaining whether we had unearthed anything of real value.

In our case, we were sifting through paid clicks, a sort of virtual trash, and our gold came in the form of customers (read: students) who might be convinced by a highly commissioned sales rep to plunk down tens of thousands of dollars for an online criminal justice certificate program that they were told, in two hours per week, would guarantee a six-figure salary. Unfortunately, reality rarely turned out that way.

As you may sense, I'm not proud now—nor was I then—of the product we sold, but I rationalized my participation as simply part of a well-rounded entrepreneurial education.

I wasn't the only one uninspired by the "lead-gen" business, but inspiration isn't what we were optimizing for. We were building a plain, boring, copycat business by design; and lesson one of my entrepreneurial education was that a plain, boring, copycat business is a great place for an entrepreneur to get an education. The fact that a lead-gen company had no barriers to entry, proven economics, and could be built by three guys in less than three months with virtually no startup capital meant it wouldn't make us famous, but it would make us money.

Businesses like ours are often condescendingly referred to as "execution plays" because they don't entail the technology risk, market risk, and business-model risk that VCs often use as a proxy for how big an entrepreneur's "big hairy audacious goal" can be. While most of Silicon Valley was swinging for the fences, we were playing "small ball"—a baseball strategy that relies on scoring runs by doing *all* the little things (e.g., drawing walks, stealing bases, sacrificing at-bats), rather than by hoping for the *one* big thing (e.g., home runs). There is nothing sexy about an entire business predicated on improving a click-through rate from 0.85 to 0.95 percent, but that was basically our mission. We found our task not nearly as easy as it sounded, so after a few failed attempts to beat the competition, we joined them. Judging by the cease-and-desist orders we received, our imitation wasn't seen as flattery, but by the time our rivals wised up to our stunt we'd racked up enough incremental improvements not to care.

Beyond those incremental improvements, we'd also racked up a fair bit of cash and we were faced with the high-class problem of what to do with it. No one at Ampush, the founders included, aspired to the lead-gen business long-term. In fact, from the out-set, we viewed lead-gen more as a financing mechanism than as a standalone business—a way to fund our "cool ideas" without ceding control to outside investors. But when it came time to decide what was "cooler" than spending our every dollar to make two or three more, we drew a blank.

Whether lead-gen chose us or we chose lead-gen is a matter of perspective. Was money corrupting our passion or creating it?

The former narrative is a more familiar one. We can all recall instances when the chase for riches made a good person bad or a happy person sad (see Ch. 1). It's why we've all been told "Follow your passion," or "Do what you love." According to this philosophy, when money is the *cause* of action, the end result is almost assured to be unpleasant. But what about when money is the *effect* of action? When we perform well and the result is money, it's possible to derive passion from the performance, not the payout. This is termed the "craftsman mindset" by Cal Newport, who argues:

> *Passion comes after you put in the hard work to become*
> *excellent at something valuable, not before. In other words, what*
> *you do for a living is much less important than how you do it.*

If you "put your head down and plug away at getting really damn good"[4] at what you do, money may or may not follow, but enjoyment certainly will. At Ampush, we were just starting to get damn good at generating leads and we were feeling a high because of it. That we ended up with a business we never actually wanted may have been because of money, but it wasn't entirely so.

One of the peculiarities of working at Ampush was the regularity with which the founders referred to themselves in the third-person. During the early days, our fates were all so interconnected that no one particularly cared who was who. In fact, we were encouraged not to be overly concerned with titles—especially our own. But as the company grew, the founders began going to great lengths to ensure that their mythos grew along with it. The founders' craving for a deep and public reverence was not undeserved, nor should it have been unexpected—after all, they named the company after themselves—but, it wasn't without consequence. While new hires were galvanized by the boldness of the Founders—now with a capital 'F'—early team members were capital-F Frustrated. Leaders we worked *with* were now leaders we worked *for*, and by explicitly raising their status they had implicitly discounted ours.

Most employees join startups—especially in their formative stages—because of the "us against the world" mindset that is rarely found in the highly politicized bureaucracies of corporate America. We'll take less pay, we'll hold lower titles, and we'll work more hours for the chance to be collaborative instead of competitive, to be creative instead of conservative, and to be unconcerned with popularity contests, pecking orders, or promotion tracks. It's not that we don't know who the boss is; we know it too well. Unlike large companies with endless layers of middle management, founder-driven organizations are void of questions surrounding "how" or "why" the top is the top. Founders—through their act of creation—garner an implicit supremacy that Joe Supervisor constantly has to justify. The surest

---

4   Cal Newport, *So Good They Can't Ignore You: Why Skills Trump Passion in the Quest for Work You Love* (New York: Grand Central Publishing, 2012).

way to break down the hierarchy in an early-stage company is to regularly remind people of it.

Yet, this is exactly what our Founders did.

Up to this point, we'd all worked harmoniously, eager to land clients, launch product, and generate revenue. Our collective desire to avoid "real jobs" by attaining some level of initial success had bred an unbreakable camaraderie between founders and employees alike. But as the Founders' growing stature came to overshadow the contributions of the early employees, the gap in our ownership, influence, and title relative to our workload, an equation that thus far we'd accepted as fair, began to seem less so. Nothing had changed—they were still the entrepreneurs and we were still the employees; but, for the first time, we felt like it.

There is nothing an early employee likes less than becoming *just* an employee—it's why we identify more closely with our order of hiring than with our actual functional role (only in Startupland will you find resumes where being "employee number [X]" qualifies as a key accomplishment). But being employee number one is like being the first pick in the NFL draft—you'll always be first, but you won't always be best (in fact, you may *never* be). Perhaps you'll get injured, surpassed by younger talent, or replaced by a savvy veteran. Perhaps you won't fit into your team's evolving game plan. Perhaps you'll simply be overlooked. How exactly your role will diminish is debatable; that it will diminish is not.

As hard as it can be for entrepreneurs to grow with their companies, it can be even harder for employees *not to*.

That founders become increasingly distant from their founding teams is a fact of life for the same reasons your group of thirteen high-school friends is now whittled down to three—they're worrying about more people with more problems that are now a higher priority than a game of beer pong with their pals used to be. Every entrepreneur overseeing an expanding organization will, at some point, be faced with difficult tasks relating to this reality: firing a friend, separating from a co-founder, demoting an early employee, or hiring over a team member. Though these situations are a natural part of growing up—like chicken pox or acne—expecting your early employees to welcome these stages, rather than resist them, will only make things worse.

How do I know this? Because at Ampush, I made things worse.

While the Founders were busy running a campaign for an election they'd already won, I started to perceive disproportionality between their upside and mine even though they weren't there any earlier, they didn't work harder, and they couldn't perform the line-level tasks necessary for the business to operate day to day. As I looked for a way to "even the score," I noticed that we were still a small team with limited role redundancies and I told myself:

> *"If I wasn't here, doing this specific role, this business wouldn't be functioning. The Founders don't know how to do any real work, so they can't step in. If I don't stay, their business is screwed. So, forget being equally valuable, I may even be more valuable than they are. But they own 40 percent and I own 2 percent. This isn't fair. Now that they have something to lose and I've established that I'm good at what I do, I'll make demands for more stock/money/ perks. They'll fear that if I leave, the business may not continue, so they'll give me what I want, even if it is insane."*

This logic can only hold for a very short period of time when a startup is established enough to show its business potential, but not yet at the point where everyone is obviously dispensable. During this phase, mature team members will understand the fragility of startup success and will remain focused on giving their all in pursuit of the mission they signed up for. They may *recognize* the entrepreneur's vulnerabilities, but they won't *exploit* them. Your immature colleagues will.

I was an immature colleague.

As the person in charge of acquiring all visitor traffic to our Web properties, I was the revenue center for our business. Without quality traffic, there would be no leads. If there were no leads, there was no revenue. If there was no revenue, there was no business. So, I was *the* most important person at Ampush—or so I told myself. I floated this logic by a few of my colleagues, and though they reinforced my position, in doing so they decided that perhaps they too were the *most* important people in the company. After all, if there were no online forms (tech) or if there were no lead buyers (sales), we also might as well pack up and go home.

So, there I was, at the center of a group of self-righteous work-er-bees—people who'd never had the audacity to do more than take a job for pay—all of us indignant that the creators of our very jobs only shared with us a small fraction of their creation.

I didn't foment a revolution, but I certainly built up a heavy back-log of resentment and helped others do the same. Jesse and Nick soon found themselves in the startup version of Lake Wobegon (Garrison Keillor's fictional town where "all the children are above average"), where to appease each early team member's perception of their value to the company they would have to give away over 100 percent of it.

To their credit, they held the line and ultimately got out of us what they needed before our work relationships became untenable. Despite winning only minor concessions, at the time I felt good about myself for representing the "little guys" to a group of "tyrant" found-ers exploiting the working class for their gain. But facing my own set of indignant, self-righteous worker-bees a few years later (we'll get to that), I recognized my behavior at Ampush as remarkably childish.

What strikes me now as nothing more than unfounded arro-gance is a phenomenon so common that psychologists have a name for it—the Better Than Average Effect (BTAE). The BTAE observes:

> *Instead of viewing themselves as average and common, most people think of themselves as exceptional and unique, especially in comparison with their peers. Among other things, most people believe they are more (a) virtuous, honorable, and moral than others; (b) capable, competent, and talented than others; and (c)*

compassionate, understanding, and sympathetic than others.
People even believe they are more human than others . . . [5]

The Founders' behavior may have triggered my need for self-enhancement, but my self-appraisal was undoubtedly skewed high.

Need proof? Five years later with 100+ employees, $20m+ in annual revenues, and a multi-billion-dollar strategic partner, the Founders are still there and I'm hardly a memory.

---

5   Jonathon D. Brown, "Understanding the Better than Average Effect: Motives (Still) Matter," *Personality and Social Psychology Bulletin* 38, no. 2 (August 2011): 209–219.

CHAPTER 4

starting
~~over~~ up

WHEN I WAS LITTLE, my mom and I would play a game. I would come home from school and cry out, "I'm hungry!"

"Do you want a piece of fruit?" she'd ask.

"No," I'd say.

"Do you want a peanut butter and jelly sandwich?"

"No."

"How about some cheese and crackers?"

"No."

"I'm done guessing—make your own damn food."

Though barely removed from Ampush, I was already "done" with unemployment. At the insistence of the same characters who'd warned me college would be the best years of my life, I had tried to commit myself to a wholehearted embrace of time off under the equally false pretense that impending adulthood would prevent me from ever taking an extended holiday again. But after a few short weeks waking without my alarm clock, coffeeing in my pajamas, and bumming around my local beach, I—like most excessively ambitious, overly aggressive, and always anxious A-type personalities—came to find that stress-free living was quite stressful. So, one evening during what should have been a relaxing dinner with my dad, I turned to him and said, "I need a job."

"Do you want to go back to Wall Street?" he asked.

"No," I said.

"Do you want to work in digital media?"

"No."

"How about going to Qualcomm?"[6]

"No."

"I'm done guessing—make your own damn job."

Anticlimactic as it sounds, this is how I came to start a company. No cold-sweat vision in the middle of the night. No "aha moment" in response to an everyday annoyance. No studied opportunity after years of industry experience.

The startup world has made a science of dressing up rather unremarkable acts of conception in romantic narratives that overlook all the boring dates, awkward conversations, and uncomfortable advances that go into love at first sight.

And, though I, too, would spin up a more moving myth when it came time to hawk my wares, the impetus for my company was a mediocre sushi dinner with my father during which I couldn't think of a single job in the entire universe I would be excited to apply for.

This may sound arrogant and smell entitled—two adjectives that have come to characterize the Millennial worker—but, I assure you it is not. Despite the flack that Millennials have taken for seeking "purpose, feedback, and personal life balance in their work," numerous studies have concluded that *"meaningful differences among generations probably do not exist in the workplace."*[7] We *all* want to perform high-quality, fulfilling work for winning organizations in an environment of inclusivity and respect. What differs across generations

---

6   Qualcomm is one of the few large technology companies headquartered in San Diego and, as such, is one of the city's largest employers of technical and business talent.

7   David P. Costanza, Jessica M. Badger, et al., "Generational Differences in Work-Related Attitudes: A Meta-analysis," *Journal of Business and Psychology* 27, no. 4 (December 2012): 375-394.

is not what makes us happy so much as whether happiness is a valid pursuit.

To me, "happy" was a new concept.

At Wharton, pursuing my career was never about happiness or balance or purpose—it was about money, plain and simple. You see, when I was seven years old, my parents divorced. Unlike the young children of most broken marriages, who spend the rest of their lives in deep therapy taking blame for their parents' fallout, I moved right on to concerning myself with how my sister and I would fund a comfortable, middle-class lifestyle in case our folks ever abandoned us the way they had each other. These concerns also happened to land me in deep therapy for the past twenty-three years, but, hey, who's counting?

My daily childhood ritual of worrying about my potential financial life without my parents evolved into my daily adulthood ritual of worrying about my financial life even with them. The most basic of my everyday fiscal decisions invoked some form of backward math designed to ensure that it wouldn't take an act of God to one day have enough money to fulfill an unassuming set of life goals—to support my family, to pay for my children's college education, to care for my parents in old age (it's no wonder that when it came time to discount cash flows, I was way ahead of the game).

My financial paranoia found fertile breeding ground at Wharton, where I was surrounded by teens and early twenty-somethings who had already made plans for a vacation home, a Ferrari and, with a bit of luck, a private jet. Despite the modest concerns that fueled my money issues, it was within the Wharton petri dish where these mutated from considerations of "enough" to preoccupations with "how much." I wish I could say someone or something did this to me, but in hindsight I have nothing but a lapse in my own consciousness to blame.

I've always been a chameleon, able to blend seamlessly into my surroundings without changing my fundamental essence. I played "pothead" with the surfers, "jock" with the lacrosse team, and "nerd" with the math geeks. During the shape-shifting of my adolescent years I never lost sight of the fact that I was acting—that by conforming to my surroundings I could someday manipulate them to my advantage. When the curtain came up, I would play my part, but when the scene ended, I always came back to center—a blond-haired, beach-loving kid with an over-reliance on his mother and an above-average IQ who wanted to live simply by the ocean with a wife and dog.

During my college years, I began to confuse my role with my reality.

Without conscious intent, I became the Wall Street commodity perennially manufactured by Wharton without defect. I was on a path that would finally put lifelong financial worries in my rear-view mirror, and that was enough to blind me to whatever misgivings I should have had about taking a job I wouldn't like, in a city where I never wanted to live, surrounded by people holding their breath for 364 days only to inhale just enough air on Bonus Day to survive until the same time next year.

Quite inconveniently, I realized the error of my ways one week before starting my Wall Street job. After graduating, I went into the woods for one month as part of a program with the National Outdoor Leadership School (NOLS). Growing up, I'd had aspirations to be a mountain guide—I always admired their ingenuity, their gratitude, and their ability to find comfort in the harshest of conditions. For thirty days I backpacked through a Wyoming blizzard, living off only what I could carry, and focusing exclusively on satisfying basic needs like food and shelter. It wasn't Mt. Everest, but it was real enough for Mother Nature to make her point. To this day, NOLS was the happiest month of my life. I came out of the wilderness on June 28, 2008. I started at Lehman on July 7th. I was dead-on-arrival.

Most people would say that my journey from high-flying corporate life to unemployment was a backward one. At the time, I wouldn't have disagreed.

From an early age, we're reminded by parents, teachers, coaches, and college advisors that we should always be moving forward, staying ahead, and learning more. But what good do we do ourselves by amassing new modes of thinking without letting go of the outdated modes they supplant? It's like driving a car in Great Britain. As big a challenge as it can be *to learn* how to drive on the left side of the road, the bigger challenge is *to unlearn* how to drive on the right.[8] The implication here is that learning is not only about acquiring new information, but about letting go of old beliefs, too.

According to modern B-school curricula, the mental models we're supposed to learn and unlearn are usually confined to sterile topics like value creation, organizational design, marketing strategy, or supply chains. Yet, in spite of what our fancy degrees may have us believe, these aren't the mental models that matter most in life *or in business*. To excel as members of society *and* of the organizations in which we spend so much of our waking lives, we can't restrict our thinking about thinking to the realm of the professional, we must expand it to the personal.

In their book *Designing Your Life*, Stanford professors Bill Burnett and Dave Evans suggest that one of the keys to a well-designed life is coherency between "who you are, what you believe, and what you do." Coherency is achieved when an understanding of critical issues related to work and its meaning—what they call your "Workview"—meshes compatibly with broader ideas about the world and how it operates—what they call your "Lifeview."[9] The Workview-Lifeview framework is a bit like the yin-yang of the modern world—seemingly contradictory forces constantly seeking a balance that, when found, creates a whole greater than the sum of its parts. When our personal and professional lives are honestly informed by one another, we will find ourselves operating at our highest levels in each.

8　This example is borrowed from a November 2016 Harvard Business Review article by Mark Bonchek titled "Why the Problem with Learning is Unlearning."

9　Bill Burnett and Dave Evans, *Designing Your Life: How to Build a Well-lived, Joyful Life* (New York: Knopf, 2016).

Taking notice of your personal life will probably strike your workaholic counterparts as listless or lazy, but that's one example of a mental model worth unlearning. Though an honest self-assessment may reveal that you've subordinated your family, your friends, or your health in a manner worthy of redress, it's also possible to find yourself doubly committed, extra enthused, and working harder to achieve a professional outcome consistent with the life you want to live. That's how I felt when I finally started my company.

It turns out that the mechanics of starting a startup are quite banal.

In my case, the only requisite ingredients were a technical co-founder, an honest lawyer, and a half-decent (read: half-baked) idea—in that order.

THE CO-FOUNDER. In my early days at Ampush, when the entire founding team was fresh off the Wharton assembly line, I committed to myself that if I ever started a company, I would have a technical co-founder.

I made Bill's acquaintance at a local "wantrepreneur" seminar—a place where aspiring founders tossed ideas against the wall in the misguided belief that startup freedom was ten short weeks and a certificate of completion away. Bill was on sabbatical from his PhD program in cognitive neuroscience and eager to trade academic torture for that of the startup variety (I'm not sure which is worse). We met a few times to discuss ideas in financial services, and after a couple meetings, I told him that if we wanted to go one step further, we needed an engineer. Fortunately, he had just the guy, Russell, who also happened to be his best friend.

Russell was a brilliant computer scientist who, like me, lasted less than twelve months in the bureaucracy of his first professional role (his was at Lawrence Livermore National Laboratory). He had moved from the Bay Area to San Diego to join a seed-stage natural language processing startup where he built algorithms to infer from a phone conversation the emotional states of its participants (ever been angry without telling the person on the other end of the line to go fuck himself?). The business was poised for success when its CEO, on a whim, decided he was better suited to corporate life, took a job at Nestlé, moved to Switzerland, and left everyone in his dust.

I came through with a vacuum cleaner at just the right time and sucked Russell into my scheme. Now, there was only one problem—Bill.

That's right. We were building a financial technology company (see: half-decent idea) and Bill wasn't particularly savvy about "fin" or "tech." Having an extra co-founder hanging around who couldn't contribute anything obvious—other than enthusiasm—would slow us down, complicate decision-making, and delay the inevitable chaos that would ensue when he would be fired, forfeit his equity, and pin Russell uncomfortably between a choice of friendship (him) and partnership (me). I couldn't let that happen.

So, after agreeing on equity splits the week prior, I invited Bill to coffee under the guise of a business meeting. I told him politely that I couldn't start the company feeling like I had the wrong team, and that there wasn't a seat for him on the bus—at least, not if I was driving. Like a nervous but resolute boyfriend soliciting the consent of his father-in-law to be, I asked Bill for his blessing to continue with Russell, knowing that, whatever his response, we were getting married. And, like a father resigned to the fact that his daughter will marry whoever the hell she wants, no matter his level of contempt, it was futile for Bill to do anything but approve.

Bill was out. Russell was in. And, we were Founders.

THE LAWYERS. It is common for most every major law firm to defer the first twenty-five to fifty thousand dollars of fees to a startup company as a way to attract businesses that may turn out to be the next Facebook. Usually, this deferral covers commodity work, such as filing incorporation papers, establishing an equity incentive plan, and documenting a seed round (a company's first round of outside investment). By the time the client needs complex (more expensive) legal work done, it will be out of its deferral period and the law firm will more than make up any potential loss from its earlier gamble.

Unlike the typical technology startup, our business—an online lender—required a bit more specialized legal work prior to launch. In addition to cookie-cutter corporate matters, we needed to deal with less commonplace topics such as a securities law, state lending licensure, and usury caps.

In San Diego I found no fewer than five law firms that tried to sell me on the breadth of their lending expertise, only to find that they didn't know more about a credit agreement than I did. Lawyers are not typically known for their business acumen, but these firms had mastered the art of selling the sizzle. Entrepreneurs tend to call this "storytelling" or "defining a vision," but in reality it is making a promise you probably can't keep, and hoping you've already cashed the checks by the time your investors figure that out.

Fortunately, every engagement letter I had signed contained a deferral arrangement. They said deferment, I heard investment. And, startup investments by their nature are illiquid and specula- tive. One by one, as the sizzle quieted only to reveal raw steak, I broke the engagements, thanked them for their investments, and subse- quently signed up with the first firm who explicitly told me what it was they *wouldn't* be able to help me with. This firm did a decent job with the corporate work and left me to find specialist counsel for lending and regulatory matters.

After churning through nearly as many lawyers in five weeks as I would employees in five years, Russell and I formed an entity and issued some stock. Though we had nothing, we each had a lot of it!

THE HALF-DECENT IDEA. Like most startups, the half-decent idea I started with wasn't the same as the failed business I ended with, but it wasn't too far afield. I left Ampush in spring 2012, as the JOBS Act—a piece of progressive financial legislation—was gaining momentum, adding crowdfunding to the techie lexicon. Crowdfunding was a simple concept—use the Internet to allow regular people to pool cap- ital for investment into previously inaccessible opportunities. These opportunities ranged from creative projects to consumer products to financial securities. The latter intrigued me the most.

Despite being a few years removed from the financial meltdown, discontent with the banking system was still at a fever pitch. As banks returned to profitability, a handful of Internet startups capitalized on a particularly populist strain of animosity that posed the following question: "Why let the bank get away with paying you almost no interest on your deposits, only to earn fat profits by loaning out your money at higher rates?" I think most financial novices understand that owning an IOU from a trillion-dollar institution with explicit and implicit government guarantees is different than owning one from Joe Blotz who, like most Americans, wants to buy something he doesn't need with money he doesn't have. But it was a poignant question at the right time. Lending Club let people buy consumer loans. Social Finance (SoFi) let people buy student loans. Funders Club let people buy seed-stage equity. Our company would let people buy small business loans. In fact, the first slide of our PowerPoint presentation read, "Small business lending without the bank."

The pitch for all of these businesses was simple. Banks are inefficient. The reason they can't pay more interest on your deposits is because they have expensive branch networks, clunky technology infrastructure, and burdensome compliance regimes. If you remove the buildings, digitize the process, and shield it from regulatory oversight—if you, effectively, remove the bank altogether—the same interest income that funds its overhead could instead fund your bank account, an especially attractive proposition with interest rates at record lows.

To grizzled, gray-haired industry veterans, this sounded like nothing more than a finance company. To inexperienced financiers like myself, this sounded revolutionary.

And, I've since learned that *sounding* revolutionary is half the battle when it comes to raising money, especially from venture capitalists. Historically, VCs have stayed away from financial services, especially capital-intensive businesses like lending. But if you build a *fintech* company to *disintermediate* the banking system with a *marketplace* model that is *balance sheet lite,* you will set off a Pavlovian response in every partner meeting west of the Mississippi.

So, we threw our hat into the ring as "the Lending Club of Small Business," offering high net-worth and institutional investors a marketplace to invest in small business loans. We set up a website, put out a press release, and, voilá, Dealstruck was born.

CHAPTER 5

what do we
do now?

AFTER INCORPORATING, Russell and I figured we might as well start showing up to work on a consistent basis. Each morning, I would arrive around 8 a.m. and, in classic engineer fashion, he would follow a couple hours later. Our office was 150 square feet of sublet space in the back corner of an Internet marketing agency that eventually became one of our customers. (In a perverse and morbid twist, our benevolent landlord would one day default on its loan with us and shut its doors, only to see its location become the new world-wide headquarters for a micro-VC firm that had provided some of the very funds they couldn't repay. Turns out that absurd stories like this are more rule than exception when good businesses go bad.) We didn't have a recipe to follow, but we'd at least found a kitchen to finish baking our still-undercooked idea and it felt good to wake up every day with somewhere to go, even if the reasons for going there weren't entirely clear.

I had expected absolute pandemonium from the moment we decided to dive fully into building our business—sixteen-hour days, non-stop negotiating, marathon coding sessions. The reality was much more mundane. Maybe it was because we were first-time entrepreneurs, but most of our early days were simply spent trying to figure out what to do next. I would read industry articles, catalog competitive offerings, and dangle the carrot of our business in front of prospective service providers to extract as much free advice as I could. Russell would brainstorm names (we hadn't yet come up with Dealstruck), work on side projects, and wait patiently for me to provide some intelligent guidance on how to proceed (he is still waiting, I think). Eventually, the pandemonium would come, but at this stage we often waited for the relief of the twelve o'clock hour when we could blend in with gainfully employed America and fuel our delusion that what we were doing qualified as work.

This anticlimax was difficult to deal with.

Launching a startup was, in many ways, like cooking rice. You crank up the heat to get the water boiling, but then immediately put it on a long, slow simmer. This left me with extra time and energy that I regretfully devoted to the counterproductive tasks of second-guessing my leap into entrepreneurship, enumerating my lack of qualifications, and ruminating on the consequences of failure.

There were only two ways to cure my mental malaise: stop or go. I chose go. So, I started filling my calendar with anyone gracious enough to spare me fifteen minutes so long as they: a) had money, b) appeared to have money, or c) had access to money. The latter two groups often wore the same cologne as group A, and, unlike the experienced entrepreneur, I was the drug-sniffing dog that couldn't discern between oregano and Aloha Kush. At the end of most meetings, I would make my ask—awaiting a simple yes or no—only to hear: "I've got a guy . . ." or "I know someone who . . ." or "We might be able to help . . ." This was the classic con—walking into a sales pitch only to realize that you are the one being sold.

The upside to these meetings was being able to refine my pitch without consequence. After enough people without money tell you why they won't give you the money they don't have, you will be fully prepared to persuade people who actually have money to give it to you. By surfacing as many tricky questions, nuanced objections, and disputed facts from audiences that can't invest even if they like what they hear, you'll eventually craft a presentation for real check-writers that preempts almost every credible rationale for rejection. That doesn't mean you won't get rejected; perhaps they'll dislike your haircut or the color of your shirt, but that's nothing a trip to Super Cuts or Nordstrom can't cure.

Unlike most startups, Dealstruck had to pursue two different investment pitches.

The initial pitch was related to lending capital. As a small business loan marketplace, we had to convince enough people of two things: first, that they could lend to the Laundromat on the corner without losing their shirt (pun intended); and, second, that doing so at 15 percent was a better idea than buying an investment-grade bond (e.g, Coca-Cola) earning 3 percent. To amass sufficient liquidity to launch our marketplace where the average loan size was $100k, we estimated needing fifty investors (dubbed Founding Lenders) willing to commit $50k across ten loans in $5k increments—so, $2.5m in total.

This process was absolutely brutal. We not only had to overcome concerns related to the *actual* risks of the loans we were marketing, but to the *perceived* risks too.

Humans are notoriously bad at estimating probabilities, largely the result of our being afflicted by a rather lengthy list of systematic cognitive biases. One such bias—known as the Availability Heuristic—suggests that we ascribe higher probabilities to events that more easily come to mind. In one famous study,[10] participants were asked to predict whether a word sampled at random from the English language was more likely to start with the letter *K* or have *K* as its third letter. The experimenters noted:

---

10 Amos Tversky and Daniel Kahneman, "Availability: A Heuristic for Judging Frequency and Probability," *Cognitive Psychology* 5 (1973): 207–232.

According to our thesis, people answer such a question by comparing the availability of the two categories … It is certainly easier to think of words that start with a K than of words where K is in the third position. If the judgment of frequency is mediated by assessed availability, then words that start with K should be judged more frequent.

The result? Though "a typical text contains twice as many words in which *K* is in the third position than words that start with *K*," nearly 70 percent of participants believed the opposite.

In our specific context—that of small business lending—most people are more likely to recall driving by a failed neighborhood restaurant, walking past a local going-out-of-business sale, or hearing about a nearby shop owner who lost it all than they are to recollect a distant corporation being unable to pay back a bond. In every game of word association I played with high net-worth investors, "risky" was always what came to mind whenever I said "small business" (it's true that small businesses are risky, they just aren't *as* risky—according to empirical data—as most people think they are). As a matter of fact, the first loan we ever offered on our platform had *already been approved* by a bank for $250,000 at an interest rate of 7 percent; yet, when I asked for feedback, most prospective investors wouldn't touch it for less than triple that.

Some will point to our outcome five years later as evidence they were right, but using future data to justify a past decision—eponymously named the Outcome Bias—is only slightly less irrational than thinking you are more likely to die in a plane than a car (the latter is 2,000x more likely).[11]

Psychological phenomena aside, the fact about raising money is that it's more than the facts that matter.

---

11   According to a July 2013 article published by *The Week*, the odds of dying in a plane crash are 11 million to 1, whereas the odds of dying in a car crash are "only" 5 thousand to 1.

Though overcoming the flawed cognitive models of potential Founding Lenders wasn't an insignificant hurdle, the challenge paled in comparison to overcoming my own mental miscalibration.

A friend of mine in the insurance business—whose sales cycle I was using as a proxy for my own—often quipped that he needed nineteen people to say "no" on the way to one "yes." This meant I'd be in for rejection 950 times before meeting my goal. That may be over-stating things, but not by much. While a good salesperson accepts "no" as part of a statistical phenomenon, I wasn't a good salesperson. "No" hurt.

To sit across from someone older, richer, and more experienced and listen while he belittles your idea, your competency, or both, and to view it through a strictly quantitative lens is not something a deeply introspective therapy patient who spends $200 per week discussing the intricacies of feelings is well-equipped to do. When they said "no," I heard, "you're not good enough," "you're not smart enough," and "you're not worth it."

In fundraising, I've found that self-avoidance is a far better strat-egy than self-analysis.

Despite the challenges, we eventually made it to our goal. In large part, this was due to a one-word tweak in the phrasing of our "ask"—instead of seeking a commitment, I now sought a "soft" com-mitment. I framed my request as a hypothetical: "If I were to bring you the Laundromat on the corner, would you consider reviewing their loan request with the intent of investing if it meets the credit criteria I've just described to you?"

This question was harmless enough to warrant an affirmative response. Then, the follow-up:

"Would you be willing to transfer $50k to a segregated, FDIC-insured bank account on our platform that you can remove anytime if you don't want to lend?"

Few people transferred $50k, but most people transferred some-thing. With the fear of commitment removed, it was harder for people to say they were interested in lending, but then to say they were uninterested in transferring money knowing they couldn't make a loan without doing so. Once funds were live on the platform and deploying capital was one click away, when it came time to decide whether to give the Laundromat its money, most Founding Lenders were past the point of no return.

As I was shaking down every Tom, Dick, and Harry in the Greater San Diego area to circle enough lending capital for launch, I was simultaneously pursuing a second pitch for seed equity.

For better or worse, I am a member of what Warren Buffett refers to as "The Lucky Sperm Club." For better, I have an entrepreneur father with the financial capacity to write a check based on love rather than logic. For worse, I have guilt over an investment I didn't earn from a parent whose success I'd probably never match. (The daddy issues are mine, not his.) So, he put up $75k, I put up $25k, and for the moment we didn't need anything else.

Having rounded up some folks willing to lend and enough seed money to pay for lunch indefinitely, I was back on a slow simmer, again asking myself, "What do we do now?"

Soon, I realized the best way to answer that question was to ask another one: "Who do we need now?"

CHAPTER 6

who do we need now?

HAVING GONE TO WHARTON and worked on Wall Street, my dubious qualifications to run a finance company were somewhat obscured, but even I couldn't trick myself into thinking I knew how to underwrite a commercial loan. To this point, my hiring experience was limited to Ampush, where my team consisted of a friend, a friend's brother, and an awkward Asian guy thrust upon me by my superiors when I was taking too long to find a suitable mate. When it comes to finding Mr. or Mrs. Right, settling for good enough isn't a great long-term strategy, but resisting an arranged marriage is hard to do.

In need of a credit expert and without a substantial professional network, I turned to the "spray and pray" approach of modern-day recruiting, logging on to LinkedIn to search for "commercial underwriter" and to send inquiries to every first, second, and third connection I had. After a few uninspiring phone calls with big-resume candidates from big-name firms (this became a common theme), I received an introduction to Steve—an ex-Marine, ex-regulator who was currently supporting his wife, his wife's tweenage sister, and a one-year-old daughter by anonymously underwriting commercial loans at an equally anonymous mid-sized regional bank. Sounds like just the type for a startup, doesn't he?

On my first call with Steve, I told him Dealstruck was going to build a big business making the best loans that banks wouldn't. Without hesitation, he rattled off two illustrative deals where banks had turned down loans he would have made. His examples were dead on, prompting me to invite him for coffee.

Meeting with Steve in person was equal parts awkward and intimidating. He wore a suit, I wore jeans; he was a dad, I was a kid; he was a Marine, I was a civilian. The contrast was stark, but that didn't bother me. What did was the fact that Steve spoke in a monotone with few facial expressions and fewer words. While I rambled on about how technology, monetary policy, and public sentiment were conspiring to create the best moment in history to be an alternative lender, he sipped on his iced vanilla latte until the only thing left was the sucking sound at the end of his straw. I think his straw spoke more than he did that day. I couldn't tell if the guy was stoic or stupid.

Toward the end our "conversation," I told Steve that I was looking for someone smart, rigorous, and committed, with solid credit fundamentals, but not beholden to bank conservatism. Finally, he spoke: "Do you think I am those things?" Given the only thing I knew for sure about Steve was his coffee preference, I should have answered (d) Not Enough Information, but instead I answered yes. After a few weeks negotiating an offer letter, Steve signed on. It was November 2012. With the holidays coming up, we targeted a start date of April 2013, timed to coincide neatly with what I hoped would be the completion of our first outside capital raise. Hire number one complete (or so I thought).

Now that I had my underwriter, I went looking to fill our other obvious vacancy—sales and marketing. This time I went the more conventional route of a referral from a known source: my stepmom, Barbara.

Barbara introduced me to Eileen, a recently failed entrepreneur who, after taking a year out of the workforce to be Mom to her two young children, was ready to get back into the startup fold. Though her prior venture never amounted to more than a few part-timers, Eileen was a walking dictionary of startup buzzwords—the first hint that she was more show than substance—and had taken an idea from concept to creation. I figured her past failure might help me avoid those missteps, so I brought her aboard. Everything through the point of hiring Eileen went smoothly, but she didn't wait for the ink to dry on her offer letter before making my life a veritable hell. Things could not have gone more wrong, more quickly, had we tried.

For one, she had clearly not reconciled her prior failure. Every day I heard a new reason why her business failed, and none of them started with "I." Despite lacking engineering expertise, she took to lecturing Russell on how he should architect his code and run his software development process. She reminded us regularly of how amazing she was—and how inadequate we were—because she was working a startup job *and* being a mom. To be productive (or maybe just to check Facebook) she needed her own office. And, finally, she craved more Fun. Fun, with a capital *F* of course, being that brand of entertainment characterized by Ping-Pong tables, Segways, kegerators, and the excessive celebration of every obscure holiday (March 23rd is Puppy Day!) that startup voyeurs often mistake as the deciding factor in why Google beat Yahoo.

The only saving grace was that after making such a terrible hire, I was relatively quick to realize I had to end it. Before doing so, however, I invited Steve to lunch shortly after the New Year to make sure Santa hadn't brought him a change of heart for Christmas. We agreed to meet again at Specialty's, the bakery that played backdrop to our first riveting dialogue.

I sat at a table for two on the far side of the restaurant, facing the parking lot. After waiting a few minutes, I spotted Steve getting out of his car. He was walking briskly, hands in his coat pockets, a strained look on his face—picture a high-school freshman who, after mustering the courage to ask his upper-class crush to Prom, was racing to recite well-rehearsed lines before he changed his mind, forgot them, or fucked them up entirely. I had a pretty good sense that Steve wasn't here to ask me to the dance. In one fluid sequence of perfect choreography Steve arrived to the table, grabbed a seat, leaned forward, said, "I'm not taking the job," turned to the side, stood up, and left without stopping. What. The. Fuck.

My first hire had to be fired and my second hire fired himself before starting. I expected hiring to be among the hardest parts of the job (anything over a 50 percent hit rate is deemed success), but even this qualified as extreme. So I did what any self-respecting first-time entrepreneur would do. I said, "Dad, help me!"

I'm not proud to have leaned on my father. Had we not shared the same last name, his guidance wouldn't have been at all different from a young CEO seeking counsel from an older, wiser, more experienced veteran. But our common gene pool has the unfortunate side effect of painting our business interactions with the embarrassing brush of nepotism. In hindsight, I'd realize I was the artist and the canvas was my imagination—that nepotism was just a tidy excuse for the sense of inadequacy that arose within me whenever I needed the Old Man's assistance.

My dad gave Steve a call and eventually brought him back to the table—something I probably wouldn't have been able to do alone. The main issue was an honest misunderstanding surrounding a few thousand dollars of compensation that Steve assumed was an intentional effort to screw him and that could only be rectified by walking out. Fortunately, Steve came to his senses after a heartfelt talk; unfortunately, this wouldn't be the last time he'd try to walk. They say old habits die hard, but when it comes to negotiating, young habits die hard, too.

As for firing Eileen, not even Dad would bail me out of that one. The first time you fire someone is a lot like the first time you break up with a girlfriend—no matter how much guidance you receive beforehand, it is awkward to initiate, uncomfortable to communicate, but pure elation the moment she walks out the door. As I prepared for D-Day, the only piece of advice running through my head on repeat was my father saying, "Don't just close the door, slam it shut." This didn't mean being rude or hostile, but rather being resolute at the decisive moment when your target seeks forgiveness, swears she can change, and promises she can make it work. That is the moment of truth. Don't think about that first kiss or that romantic anniversary getaway. You are here for a reason. The door is slightly ajar. Don't just close it. Slam it shut.

I didn't.

I asked Eileen to join me for coffee one morning at 10 a.m., a relatively innocuous request given that she had made Latte Break a daily ritual (no wonder she was so busy!). We sat down and ordered, after which I said, "Eileen, this really doesn't seem to be working out."

Surprisingly, she agreed. But her solution was different. She pondered aloud, "I really don't know how we can build the business with Russell. He is impossible to work with."

I told her that Russell would be here to stay. She responded, "So what do you suggest we do?"

Now was the moment, slam it shut. But instead, I said, "Why don't you go home for a couple days to think through whether you can be here."

"Are you firing me?"

"Well, umm, I guess I think it is best if you aren't here anymore." By now my coffee was cold, so I stood up and left.

Heart racing, I called one of my advisors as I paced around the block. "Cliff, I just fired Eileen. I think. Actually, I'm not sure. Here is what I said . . . Did I fire her? Do I need to fire her again? Do you think she got the message?"

To Eileen's credit, she went home, came back that night to grab her stuff, and left her office keys on my desk. She could have humiliated me to make a point, but she didn't; I'm grateful she exited as gracefully as she did under the circumstances. The good news is that I wouldn't make this mistake again. Firing is never fun—your team members' failures are your failures—but, the pain of leaving the door propped open is worse for everyone than slamming the damn thing shut.

After twenty minutes of circling our office building, I climbed the stairs to our second-floor command center where I found waiting in the entryway our newest angel investor—also now our Board Chairman—whose wire had cleared less than twenty-four hours prior. He was here to take the four of us to lunch. One problem: now we were three.

Zalman, welcome to Dealstruck.

CHAPTER 7

the
z man

AFTER ATTENDING A PITCH COMPETITION in which I spent the first of my allotted eight minutes trying to remember my opening line (needless to say, I didn't win), I received a cryptic email from a man who identified himself only as Z. It read:

> *Over the past 20 years or so, I've started 4 companies, 3 of them in commercial finance. During that span, I've financed in the neighborhood of $6 billion to small businesses. I'm an angel investor . . . If you think I can help you, let me know.*

Given that I hadn't started any companies, let alone one in commercial finance, and that I hadn't loaned a single dollar to small businesses, "think" was the understatement of the century. I *knew* he could help me. But after spending six months convincing anyone emitting the faintest whiff of money to meet with me, I had become a bit suspicious of those asking me to meet with them. I chalked it up to the fact that Z's focus area—seed-stage ventures at the intersection of commercial finance and technology in North San Diego County—was so narrow that Dealstruck was perhaps his only hope of deploying capital, so I took the bait.

Z, short for Zalman, was the entrepreneurial opposite of my father: quietly confident, calm, soft-spoken, unhurried, and introspective. The startup world moves fast, the bullets are always flying, and Z was like Neo from the Matrix—someone who could slow time down to elegantly sidestep the most fatal of threats, all while enjoying a cup of warm tea and a chocolate croissant (he had a notorious sweet-tooth). His latest fancy footwork involved exiting his role as a part-owner and chief executive of a local factoring company after an irreconcilable dispute with his partners. Under his leadership, the company (eCapital) grew by more than 100x from a no-name mom-and-pop to the dominant player in freight factoring, profitably buying nearly $1b of invoices each year by employing big data before it was Big Data. Z saw technology as the future of commercial finance. His partners didn't. He was outnumbered, so he took his ball and went home (with a buyout from his partners in hand).

Right before our first meeting, Z had become involved with a handful of early-stage commercial fintech companies where he was The Money and The Brains, but where the execution was entrusted to key lieutenants from his life as an operator (before eCapital, he founded and sold a franchise lender, ran various commercial lending efforts at Heller Capital, and built Shell Oil's global finance arm). His investment model was simple: to provide capital and high-touch (i.e. hands-on) advisory to bring to life the ideas his previous partners rejected, but to leave the "thankless racket" of CEO-ing to people with more youth, energy, and commitment—and naiveté—than he.

Though I was under the impression Z had started three companies in commercial finance, it turned out that his definition of "start" was a bit fuzzy.

His franchise finance company was backed from the beginning with plentiful amounts of low-cost capital from Deutsche Bank. I would later come to know Z's former partner at the German bank—a gentleman by the name of Doug—who thought *he* had started the franchise lending business and merely hired Z to run it (as with my story, everyone has his own truth). At Shell Capital, Z built and led globally the growth of a $4.5b portfolio, but he had the resources of a multi-billion-dollar enterprise with a triple-A balance sheet to support his efforts. eCapital was already a profitable, going concern—though minuscule—when he bought a portion of it and spent eight years building a $75m portfolio using the owners' capital and retained earnings.

No doubt, his track record was impressive. But the plain reality was that he always had the benefit of deep-pocketed partners and never had to deal with venture money and its attendant pressures and imperatives. As a result, when it came to things like cap tables, financings, and stock grants—the ABC's of the startup world—our respective experience (approximately none) was relatively commensurate. Though we'd end up seeing eye-to-eye on most things operational during our time at Dealstruck, the financing realm was always a sticky one for us.

The first major financing initiative Dealstruck launched was in response to our decision to move from a marketplace model—a fee business originating loans for sale to outside investors (think mortgage broker)—to a direct lending model in which we retained the loans and their accompanying credit risk on our balance sheet in hopes of capturing the spread between the interest rate we charged our borrowers and the cost of our own funding (think bank). The latter model is more capital intensive, but also more profitable, and we believed it was the only long-term sustainable model for the types of loans we made.

To become a direct lender, we needed two things immediately: 1) a lending license, and 2) lending capital.

Getting licensed is easy, but takes time. Luckily, Z had a previous investment in MyBusinessLoan.com (MBL)—a company run by one of his former trusted lieutenants, Patrick, whose hair count was a reasonable proxy for his business acumen. He was bald. While Patrick was a clear-cut liability (I would practice my door slamming on him in a few months), MBL had a lender's license and Z saw an opportunity to enhance his investment by throwing it together with Dealstruck.

We hired a lawyer to generate a holding company that would own Dealstruck and MBL, and redrew the cap table (the document detailing who owns what) in the only way that I knew for certain was incorrect—equally. Z felt strongly that he, my dad (our other Board member at the time), and I own the business in identical proportions so that if the shit hit the fan, each of us would care as much as the other about supporting the company—they with money and me with sweat. This was a vestige of his time at eCapital where, rather than having outside investors, the partners were the sole funding source and where clearly defined carrots and sticks were required to prevent one of them from running for the hills in tough times. This wasn't the cheapest or the easiest way to acquire a license—nor was it the cheapest or easiest way to structure a company—but it was the fastest.

With a lenders' license in hand, we turned our attention to the other thing we needed to transition from a marketplace to a direct lender: our own capital to lend.

There are two main ways a company can raise capital.

The first way is to borrow. When a company borrows money, it issues an IOU (usually a promissory note or a bond) to its lenders, promising to repay principal and interest subject to a contractually negotiated agreement. The big upside to borrowing is the ability to use someone else's money to create value without having to share it with them (other than paying interest). But the big downside—and I mean *big*—is that borrowed money has to be repaid. If you fail to do so, your company could quickly become your lender's.

The second way to raise money is to sell ownership, referred to as "equity." When a company raises equity, it sells shares of stock at an agreed upon price (the "valuation") in an amount sufficient to generate the desired cash proceeds (for example, if a company wants to raise $10m and the price per share is $1, it would sell 10 million shares). Together, the dollar amount raised and the valuation of the company determine the percentage ownership of the new investors. Every time a company raises equity, its existing owners—who own 100 percent of the pie prior to the first raise—will end up owning a proportionally smaller percentage, since they are now sharing the pie with the new folks at the table. This process is known as "dilution."

Owning a smaller percentage doesn't necessarily mean the value of what you own has decreased—in fact, it's often the opposite. As long as the value of the business ends up growing by more than the amount of dilution, your ownership will be smaller when measured in percentages, but not when measured in dollars. The question commonly posed to make this point goes as follows: Would you rather own 100 percent of the corner deli or 2 percent of Google? Since the startup world is betting on billion-dollar exits and not on bologna sandwiches, taking dilution—even at a heavy cost—is usually the right bet.

But Z didn't see it this way.

From our first conversation, Z had hinted at his aversion to dilution when he told me that owning less than 10 percent of the company wasn't "worth his while." Thus, as our growing business needed additional equity capital, he regularly preferred to invest more of his own money, rather than to dilute his ownership stake.

In an effort to have his cake and eat it too (remember his sweet-tooth?), Z proposed that rather than raise equity to make our first batch of loans—the typical course for a startup lender—we instead issue debt. As you may recall from our earlier financing primer, the benefit of borrowing is that the upside is yours to keep. The downside, simply put, is death.

A reflection on death courtesy of my favorite comedian, Jerry Seinfeld:

> *A recent survey stated that the average person's greatest fear is having to give a speech in public. Somehow this ranked even higher than death, which was third on the list. So . . . at a funeral, most people would rather be the guy in the coffin than have to stand up and give a eulogy.*

We weren't at a funeral (yet), but if we were to end up at one, it struck me that Z would rather be in the casket than have to take dilution.

The debt instrument we structured was, for the most part, straightforward. In exchange for $10m to be used exclusively for and secured entirely by small business loans, Dealstruck agreed to pay 12 percent interest per annum. As additional inducement to outside participants, Z, my dad, and I (to a lesser extent) invested $2m (of the $10m), agreeing also to absorb losses on our investment first. In technical parlance, we were "subordinate." In plain English:

> "More than 20% of the loans we make will have to go bad before you lose any money. And, if you lose any money, we will have lost all of ours first."

With loan losses expected to be only 5 percent, getting paid 12 percent every year *and* being protected for losses as high as 20% seemed like quite a deal.

But there was one twist.

Just like we would subordinate our $2m to the remaining $8m, the instrument on offer required that participants also agree to subordinate in the future to yet another lender, known as a "senior lender." In plain English:

> "We're at the bottom of the stack now, but eventually you'll be right there with us."

If the current stack was our $2m protecting their $8m, it was safe to assume the future stack could be our collective $10m protecting a senior lender's $40m. As the total size of the stack increased, the amount of pain it would take for those at the bottom to start feeling it would decrease (losing 20 percent of $10m is the same as losing just 4 percent of $50m). And, with capital markets the way they were in 2014, adding $40m to our stack would be about as difficult as getting laid on J*Date—easy.

Given this subordination feature, I took to calling this $10m instrument our Sub Debt and, for the better part of seven months, I ran around town with Sub Debt for sale until I had finally corralled an additional $8m from thirty-one of my closest friends. Though I specifically highlighted the possibility of future subordination—the proverbial fine print—to every single investor I pitched, their general response was, "Yeah, sure, whatever. Where do I sign?"

I can't blame the Sub Debt investors for overlooking the ramifications of "the twist." In all honesty, I didn't fully grasp its significance, either, back then, and, if I had, I'm not sure I would have been able to market it in good faith.

I remember having a gut sense that certain financing strategies we were pursuing were likely to end badly; that a fragile, early-stage company shouldn't already be involved in such complex financial engineering. But I lacked conviction and confidence in my intuition, when I needed it most, to overrule Z and his twenty-five years doing successfully exactly what it was we were planning to do.

First-time CEOs face a particularly difficult balancing act when weighing their instincts against the counsel of investors—both current and prospective—who presuppose, by virtue of their investment, that their guidance is as valuable as their money.

Investors are keen to find entrepreneurs who are "coachable" (which can be code for "they do what I say"). To demonstrate this trait, the first-timer is encouraged to surround himself with directors, advisors, and mentors, and to display a level of deference that demonstrates humility, self-awareness, and intellectual honesty. This is sensible to a point, but if you aren't careful you could find yourself in a situation where you're unable to order breakfast without convening a conference call to debate the relative merits of pancakes versus French toast.

Experienced entrepreneurs, wary of reaching that point, will tell you to keep your walls appropriately high. They know firsthand that the founder's pheromone has a tendency to attract uninformed opinions from a class of professionals who have chosen to stand safely on the sideline, doling out unsolicited advice to satisfy their need to feel part of something courageous and brave. Their thoughts are offered not for your benefit, but for their own—and the input will only introduce unnecessary distraction, delay, and doubt. Making sure they don't breach your barriers is paramount.

If Zalman planted a few bad seeds, it was my mistake to bring a watering can when I should have brought Weed-B-Gone. The constant battle to differentiate valuable guidance from glorified guesswork is hard enough, let alone when the same person is providing half of each. However, I had already classified Z as someone worthy of being on my side of the wall and, while I harbored reservations about his approach to financing, I ultimately decided his age, money, and experience to be more reliable than my hunch.

The Sub Debt itself wasn't doomed to fail, but its structure was fundamentally too weak for the building we intended to erect atop it. Maybe an earthquake wouldn't hit, everyone would make it out alive, and we'd be vindicated by selling our skyscraper for a sky-high number before the bottom fell out. But in startups, and especially in *lending* startups, the bottom falling out isn't uncommon. Those who start on the bottom—the equity—know this and consciously trade high risk for high reward. Those who don't—the debt—expect to be repaid even if the ground shakes. As you pile more layers of debt onto a business, what used to be the penthouse suite eventually becomes the mail room—and, our Sub Debt investors weren't here to lick stamps.

The motive for all of this wheeling-and-dealing was simple: grow the value of Dealstruck without decreasing our ownership interests.

Dilution was coming eventually—we all knew this. But, the approach we took was to push "eventually" as far into the future as possible so when it came time to share the pie, we were selling slices at a valuation of $50m instead of $5m. Once we were that far down the runway, we'd take some proceeds from our bake sale, pay off the Sub Debt (including our own), and leave the rest of dessert to the equity—which we would still own most of.

To pave this runway to riches, Z not only poured more of his money into the equity, but he poured it into the Sub Debt as well. In the spirit of equality, he expected my father to match—a feasible ask knowing his war chest was the bigger of the two (remember, Lucky Sperm Club). Despite my best efforts (yes, I actually pitched them *not* to invest more), both men ended up with an unnecessarily large chunk of net-worth on the line and I ended up shouldering the unnecessarily heavy burden of making sure it got back to them.

(Note to self: don't take investment from people who don't fully understand there is a reasonably high probability they may lose *all* of it.)

The plan we put into action may sound incredibly complex, extremely convoluted, and, well, borderline crazy, but in spreadsheet form its mathematical elegance might evoke different descriptors— efficient, optimized, lean.

During one of my early venture meetings, I remember being told, "We like you, we like your traction, but we just don't like spreadsheet businesses."

Spreadsheet businesses, I would learn, are that genre of enterprise for which a plausible plan can be easily engineered on paper, but that almost never pans out in practice. Finance companies— online or not—are a case in point. The difference between a $10b company and a $10m company (or even a worthless company) can hinge on minute shifts in pricing, acquisition costs, loss rates, or overhead. On a spreadsheet, overlooking the exponential difficulty of achieving small tweaks in assumptions is too easy to do. The question is not whether the spreadsheet has to work—in the long run it must for *every* business. The question is how easy is it to believe the assumptions that make it work. It's unlikely that investment committee meetings about flying cars, drone delivery networks, or miracle drugs need to revolve around percentage point changes in an Excel model, but those regarding finance companies probably do.

Our scheme was a spreadsheet bet—a gamble that the business would come to life exactly as modeled, with everything going right.

We'd pushed our chips all-in, I'd convinced thirty-one Sub Debt investors to join us, and we were off to make (pipe) dream reality . . . almost.

There is one detail I neglected to mention earlier. When Dealstruck took over MBL, we didn't solely inherit Patrick. We also inherited another of Z's loyal associates—a man by the name of Rudy. He had worked with Z for fifteen years, first as an underwriter at his franchise finance company and, more recently, as head of portfolio risk management at his factoring business. Rudy was Z's secret weapon—a sort of Swiss Army knife executive that knew credit, operations, and technology, and that over the course of his career had touched nearly every non–real estate asset in commercial finance. Unlike Patrick, Rudy had real skills, and since I trusted Z and Z trusted Rudy, I figured I ought to trust Rudy, too.

But the transitive property doesn't apply to trust. Hiring on the basis of a referral is one thing, but trusting on that basis is another. Obvious as it seems, "Hirer Beware!" When you are studying a strong resume from a big-time referral source it may be harder than you expect to remember that past performance is not indicative of future results.

Now, remember Z's modus operandi—to find hands-on operators like me to bring his ideas to life. Well, he had one more big idea for which Rudy was a critical ingredient. Prior to becoming an angel investor, Z ran a factoring company[12] where Rudy was his top operator. There, Rudy and Z had ginned up a new product idea, a casualty of the aforementioned irreconcilable dispute between Z and his partners. Dealstruck provided them the perfect platform to revive it. So, in addition to vanilla term loans (think of a mortgage or auto loan—lump-sum borrowing paid back in monthly installments), we

---

12   Factoring is a form of receivables finance whereby businesses that are owed money from their customers can sell the receivable at a discount in exchange for immediate cash. For small businesses with limited cash, factoring can be a lifeline (irrespective of cost) relative to waiting thirty or sixty days to get paid. We'll get into some details later, but suffice it to say that receivables finance is a highly specialized form of financing in which neither I nor my existing team had any experience.

decided that Dealstruck would also offer credit lines to help business owners accelerate cash from their accounts receivable.

Warren Buffett—the famed billionaire investor—attributes much of his success to staying within his "circle of competence." In a world where bigger is almost always deemed better, Buffet offers a contrarian view: "The size of that circle is not very important; knowing its boundaries, however, is vital."

The truth is I went out of bounds. I had no business leading a company involved in the highly specialized world of receivables finance.

But the paradox for the first-time entrepreneur is this: you don't have any business leading a company at all. I had never hired a team before, but I did. I had never raised money before, but I did. I had never launched a product before, but I did. The first-time entrepreneur's history is littered with obstacles overcome as they arose. Everything is a first. Everything is unknown. Where do you draw the line?

I thought I had followed The Rules: I had an experienced Executive Chairman (Z) and I had smarter people than me at the table (Rudy)—so I went ahead with the new product. It was September 2013—we were licensed, we were capitalized, and, now, we were unique. In calendar years, we had just turned one (though my hairline would have suggested otherwise), but the business was just now beginning.

CHAPTER 8

CAN
it be?

THE FIRST THREE QUARTERS of the following year were mostly characterized by business as usual, which, for me, consisted almost exclusively of raising debt and equity like a perfectly honed just-in-time inventory (JIT) management system.[13] During this time period, we never had more than ninety days of operating cash on-hand and, more than once, the newest of my Sub Debt recruits wired funds minutes before our account struck zero, saving me from the thoroughly emasculating task of admitting to our clients that we were out of money (which, by extension, probably meant they'd soon be out of money, too).

When it comes to managing cash, I highly recommend against anything that resembles just-in-time. This is especially true in a lending business where cash is nothing more than inventory. It is, quite literally, the only thing we sell. Have you ever been to a sandwich shop only to find out that they've run out of bread? I have. And, my reflex reaction is to make a snide remark about the idiocy of a business owner who can't figure out how to keep in stock the only damn thing he really

---

13   Just-in-time (JIT) is an inventory strategy companies employ to increase efficiency and decrease waste by receiving goods only as they are needed in the production process, thereby reducing inventory costs. This method requires producers to forecast demand accurately. (Thanks, Investopedia!)

needs. Ironic, isn't it? The tank never did run empty that year, but it was way too close for comfort and simply luck that Manna rained from Heaven at my precise moment of need and not one minute after.

The other big problem with JIT in a lending company—especially an early-stage one—is that a number of people at the operational level need access to bank accounts in order to disburse funds to clients, post cash collections, and perform various other reconciliation activities. I could wave my arms to convince my employees we had plenty of operating capital even when we didn't.[14] But "Don't worry, it's under control" doesn't go far when anyone with a working knowledge of arithmetic sees fifty thousand dollars in the funding account with one hundred fifty thousand teed up to wire out. If I was going to get caught with my pants down, more than a few of my team would already have their soda and popcorn ready.

In an effort to bring more certainty to our liquidity situation, I started hunting for our first institutional capital relationships in the middle of that year. Until now, most of our loan funding had been provided by rich people and a wild-man fund manager named Brendan who was grandfathered in to his position as a loan buyer, a holdover from our marketplace days. Before we could build our loan portfolio in a meaningful way, we needed larger credit facilities to ensure we would have ample access to cash to meet growing borrower demand.

Most of my hunting took place in the objectionable world of the trade show. I don't like noise, I don't like crowds, and I don't like small talk. When it came to these events, the near-perfect inverse correlation I observed between company success and CEO attendance motivated me more toward greatness than a stock grant ever could. But beggars can't be choosers.

----

14   In early-stage finance companies, lenders typically earmark their funds specifically for use in originating loans, which then serve as their collateral. This is known as "asset finance" and any cash on hand owing to a lender is commonly referred to as "restricted cash." Operating capital is funded by equity investors who become owners in the business. Their cash is "unrestricted." While some portion of it may also go toward funding loans, the vast majority is for payroll, marketing, rent, and other costs associated with ongoing operations.

It is hard to believe that any value can be derived from events where the main draw for most attendees is free food, unlimited coffee, and the chance to apply their notoriously abused per-diem to Jack Daniel's and the faint probability of getting laid.

They are, however, a necessary evil. Allow me to demonstrate.

When I started Dealstruck, there was a competitor nearly two years ahead of us called SoMoLend, led by a blond firecracker named Candace Klein. Candace never met a microphone she didn't like. She was a public relations dynamo in an industry filled with math nerds and Excel jockeys (like yours truly), which allowed her to seize the lead role in the small business lending show. For a while, she won pitch competition after pitch competition, dominated industry events, and made headline news in publications ranging from the *New York Times* to *Forbes*. We figured SoMoLend was light-years ahead of us, but we soon learned there wasn't much more beneath the surface than a cadre of interns, a handful of loans, and a looming legal battle with the State of Ohio (apparently her attention-grabbing had grabbed some attention from the wrong folks).

As the Ohio legislature's unfounded witch-hunt was putting SoMoLend out of business, the Golden Girl (literally, her hair was gold) was looking for a home. Her search led Z and me to a coffee shop adjacent to the San Diego Airport for a meeting scheduled under the exclusive guise of "Friendraising"—her cryptic way of saying, "I need a job." As an entrepreneur with a mild case of social anxiety and a staunch disdain for self-promotion, Candace was just what I needed.

Candace's main task was a daunting one—to make me charming.

The idea was to combine my substance with her sparkle to give Dealstruck a fighting chance to stand out from more than three hundred alternative lending startups vying for the attention of the same dozen venture capital firms. A witty soundbite, a memorable panel performance, or a flattering mention in an industry rag can spell the difference between getting funded or going broke. This is the Butterfly Effect—startup style.

Candace organized a rigorous public relations boot-camp during which I pitched, paneled, demoed, and interviewed until she had polished off enough tarnish to turn me into the shiny object that journalists, investors, and corp dev execs adore. I couldn't hold character for more than thirty minutes, but in a world where multi-million-dollar decisions are made on an elevator ride, that was more than enough time. Working with Candace wasn't always easy—she could laugh, cry, insult, admire, break up, and make up all in the span of a single five-minute conversation—but, she truly was one of the best in the business when it came to creating buzz.

The first conference I spoke at wasn't much of a conference at all (as with investors, practice on the ones you don't care about). It was a sparsely attended event focused on debt crowdfunding held in New York City the week before Christmas in the middle of a snowstorm—"location, location, location" be damned! Z and Candace were kind enough to accompany me, and while I was busy sweating through my undershirt preparing to take the stage, the two of them got to working the room. After my panel—I remembered my lines, but my performance was otherwise forgettable—Candace introduced me to a middle-aged woman with a kind smile named Amy who was a writer for the *New York Times*. There weren't many CEOs in attendance, but Amy didn't want to leave empty-handed, so she asked me for an interview. Tedious as it may have been for her, for me it was quite a privilege to be a slow news day away from a mention in "All the News that's Fit to Print." Amy wasn't looking for a story—just for industry insight—but, this was the *New York f'ing Times!* So, I decided I'd speak to her until she had exhausted her question bank, no matter how long it took. (It took slightly over one hour.)

I figured I'd never hear from Amy again. But three months later, we were on the front page of the *New York Times* business section. The story, featuring one of our earliest clients, may have been the single most important factor in making Dealstruck a relevant player. When I asked Candace why Amy featured Dealstruck when there were plenty of other larger, heavily funded brand names to choose from, she said it was because I didn't treat her with the condescension, paternalism, and self-importance that most other male executives in financial services did. I wasn't acting—insecurity and humility often go hand-in-hand—but, Candace's Charm School sure didn't hurt.

Following my initial conversation with Amy, Z did his part by introducing me to a curly-haired gentleman with a head slightly too large for his body that I recognized as having sat directly behind us in the audience. His name was Glenn and he was the former CEO of CAN Capital, the largest subprime small business lender in the country (subprime is an umbrella term for the broad cross-section of borrowers with less-than-perfect credit who, because of their risk-profile, are often forced to borrow at exorbitant rates from non-bank lenders). Glenn was fresh off a twelve-year stint at CAN and, like Z, was looking for interesting opportunities in fintech. Dealstruck and its search for the mid-prime market—an attempt to isolate the best of the worst credits and to deliver better financing options to them—was, apparently, interesting.

After a few failed attempts to bring Glenn aboard as an Advisor, due to my insistence that he write a small check to align himself with the consequences of his advice, we agreed that simply being friends was a perfectly fine equilibrium for our relationship.

As with Amy, I figured that outside of incidental run-ins at industry events, I wouldn't be hearing much from Glenn and that since he had no upside in Dealstruck, goodwill wouldn't be sufficient motivation for him to make any grand gestures in our favor.

Again, I was wrong.

In July 2014—seven months after my first conference, on the heels of steady PR buzz—Glenn called to ask if he could introduce me to the new CEO of CAN Capital. I'm no rocket scientist, but it took me approximately .26 seconds to catch his drift—CAN wanted to buy us.

While our underlying business was doing quite well (we were twenty people originating over $3m per month in new loans), let's tell each other the truth: We were about to receive an acquisition offer from an industry giant because I shook two hands at a small-time trade show that I was certain would be a waste of time. In entrepreneurship, it's not hard to be humbled.

The beauty of receiving an early acquisition offer is that a lot is still left to the imagination. As the renowned early-stage investor Josh Kopelman once said, "There's nothing like numbers to fuck up a good story." Even the most compelling vision can't escape crashing to reality the moment its hockey stick growth curve—the classic up-and-to-the-right trajectory of any forecast worth its salt—more closely resembles a stretcher. This phenomenon is exacerbated in lending where good numbers—e.g., new loan volume—come far before bad numbers—e.g., defaults (which, in our world, peaked twelve to eighteen months later). When CAN approached us, we had been originating for ten months, which was long enough to prove we could find people willing to take our money, but not so long that we'd found people unwilling give it back.

After ironing out a non-disclosure agreement (NDA),[15] Z and I flew to New York where CAN's CEO, a gentleman named Dan, used every word except "acquire" to tell us he wanted to do exactly that. I've found that direct communication is frowned upon in grown-up circles. You don't acquire, you combine. You don't fire, you separate. And, no matter how happy you are, you don't dare fucking smile. Be cool. "Thanks, Dan. We appreciate your interest. There could be something to do here. Let's keep exploring."

CAN's interest in Dealstruck was mainly aesthetic, relating directly to its planned IPO. Though CAN was the pioneer of a wildly successful, high-yield, daily-payment product known as merchant-cash advance (MCA) and though it was the reigning giant among alternative small business lenders, its limited technology infrastructure was weighing down its value in the eyes of the investing public. In order to show the stock market it could fend off the techie upstarts that had been firing arrows in its back, CAN had to demonstrate a serious commitment to technology and it had to do so fast.

---

15 Non-disclosure agreements (NDA) are legal documents that govern the use or distribution of confidential or proprietary information.

Buying us was merely a "check the technology box" exercise on the road to IPO—still a stretch given the nascent state of our software. This type of transaction is often dubbed "strategic"—as opposed to "financial"—which is a cover-your-ass term used by executives and investment bankers that loosely translates to "we're not sure what we're buying and we probably overpaid." If you are going to be acquired, try for the strategic variety.

Here's why.

For an unprofitable company that had raised $3.5m of equity and whose systems capabilities hadn't evolved far beyond processing payments on term loans (remember this), it would have been tough to make a financial argument that we were worth much more than the capital invested—$10m soaking wet. But CAN was doing different math. They were trying to go public.

In most industries, and particularly in specialty lending, public companies are valued as a multiple of earnings. Every so often, however, an industry comes along that is so in favor—so scalding hot—that the value of companies within it unhitches entirely from any sensible underlying financial metric. Fintech, at that time, was that industry. So, rather than worry about silly things like profits and book value (in accounting terms, assets less liabilities), investors solely concerned themselves with growth and scale as measured by top-line revenue, of which CAN was doing $400m per year. If acquiring Dealstruck provided a small boost to their valuation multiple—now based on annual revenue—of even an extra quarter-turn (.25x), it would be worth $100m to them. Viewed through that lens, paying $25–35m doesn't sound crazy.

And that's exactly what they were prepared to do.

The offer from CAN was for $33m—$13m in cash and $20m in pre-IPO stock. Our choice was between selling, which would eliminate our risk, but also our control and upside, and financing, which would do the opposite (we had reason to believe we could raise capital at a similar valuation).

Early in our relationship, Z taught me that there are only two rules in lending, but that they follow a very specific hierarchy: Rule

#1—Don't lose money; Rule #2—Make money. Even in a business whose sole credo is to manage downside first, it's pretty easy to get confused when you can finance your billion-dollar dream on the same terms at which you could sell it outright (one billion being the silly magic number in Silicon Valley beneath which everything is viewed as a Jiffy Lube). While your fellow Board members wouldn't be remiss if they evaluated the merits of an acquisition offer by the number of zeros it contained, you—the entrepreneur (especially the first-timer)—have something else to consider: the *Win*.

Different people define the Win differently, but for me it's quite simple—did you return more money than was invested in the business? That may seem like a low bar, but in a game show where 70 percent of the contestants go broke, giving investors a few years of excitement and their money back seems parade-worthy. The Win is the entrepreneur's lifetime membership card to an exclusive club where the main reward is the high probability of being financed again. Whether that's really a reward is something I'll let you decide.

Here's where the Board came out: Zalman wanted to sell. He'd been in specialty finance too long to pass up the chance to exit a highly cyclical, highly risky business at a time when venture firms were pushing valuations to absurd levels. My dad, cursed with entrepreneurial optimism, leaned toward passing, but was ultimately indifferent. So, it was up to me.

Though the thought of selling was bothersome—especially to CAN, where the culture wasn't better than what you'd find at your local DMV—my pros-cons table was tilted heavily in that direction. While I could easily list nearly a dozen reasons to sell, I could only find one in favor of financing: ego. And, that wasn't a good enough reason for me.

Thus, for $33m in cash and stock the Board was decided—offer accepted.

Well, not exactly.

At the time of the offer, our loan portfolio was almost $15m, most of it having been funded by—you guessed it—the Sub Debt.

As a precondition to its purchase, CAN required that it pay off our high-cost Sub Debt (12%) with its own much less costly capital (4%). This meant Sub Debt investors would get all of their money back now—a good thing—but none of the 12 percent interest they would have earned had the debt remained outstanding until its maturity date two years later—arguably, a bad thing.

CAN's ask was, on its surface, uncontroversial, except for one minor detail: Dealstruck did not have the right to prepay the Sub Debt without consent of the noteholders. And, ironically, the most reluctant noteholder was the same person who was also the staunchest advocate of the deal—Z. Though a sale to CAN would generate a 5x return on his equity in less than two years, Z wasn't interested in taking back his Sub Debt early to make that very sale happen. He figured if we pushed back hard enough, we might be able to jam CAN—a strong, stable company—into paying the high interest rate of Dealstruck—a weak, unstable company—until the Sub Debt matured. In technical terms, this is called an arbitrage; in non-technical terms, a fantasy.

So, on a Sunday night in mid-October, there was a phone call.

In one corner, Dealstruck, represented by Z and me. In the other corner, CAN, represented by Dan and his general-counsel-acting-business-partner (a clear oxymoron). The matter at hand: how to "share the pain" on the Sub Debt such that CAN could prepay it, giving the acquisition a pathway to completion.

Aside from a few minutes of the ceremonial "how's the weather" niceties, what ensued was a sixty-minute pissing match between Dan and Z that had everything to do with the size of their respective genitals and nothing to do with the size of the acquisition.

It was the only time in four years I ever saw Z yell.

After the call, Z admitted that he didn't know why he was yelling or how he got so riled up. He said Dan "hit a nerve." He entered the ring wanting to be rich, but when the bell sounded he acted as if being king was more important. In trying to be both, we ended up neither. I knew the deal was dead.

In fairness to Z, it should never have come to this.

Growing up, my father warned me about the graveyard of entrepreneurs that missed opportunities to be acquired early, only to find themselves six feet under a few short years hence. He would recount the stories of these sorry souls with faintly detectable Schadenfreude since he believed most of their funerals were the result of greed, arrogance, or some other psychological defect they couldn't suppress in favor of "rational man behavior." He was a serial entrepreneur whose success was built on small wins, and he was not shy about his disdain for the perverse, swing-for-the-fences mentality afflicting many a venture-backed entrepreneur when Fuck You Money (a crude term for wealth sufficient for financial independence) was staring them in the face.

That I couldn't find a solution to get the deal done was a failure of foresight, imagination, and courage on my part. I could have interjected on the call. I could have involved the other Sub Debt holders earlier. I could have generated a more compelling argument for the benefits of prepayment. This is the job of the CEO, and I didn't do my job. Like the other objects of my father's mockery, I was marching toward my own burial.

So, what if we had sold to CAN? Though the journey would have been different, the destination wouldn't have been. In December 2016, less than two weeks after Dealstruck closed its doors, a headline flashed across my screen, "CAN Capital puts CEO on Leave." The article exposed how CAN was forced to stop originating new loans after it lost $9m overnight due, supposedly, to systems deficiencies.

The problem?

> *The problem, sources said, is that technology the company designed to track merchant cash advances sometimes fails to properly account for term loans.*[16, 17]

---

16   "Small Business Lender Unwinds Securities." Asset-Backed Alert. Dec. 9, 2016.

17   In July 2017, CAN Capital was recapitalized with new investors, but not before laying off more than 50 percent of the company and going seven months without originating a single loan.

CHAPTER 9

series
a (not) okay

WHEN THE DEAL with CAN fell through, I went back to the Sisyphean task of fundraising. The CEO may be at the top of the org chart, but there is nothing like repeatedly pushing the weight of employee livelihoods, investor expectations, and public pressure uphill to make you feel like the bottom person on the totem pole. Though many entrepreneurs thrive on the perception of being in control, my experience was that it didn't take anything more than a convertible note[18] and a press release before my company was controlling me. I rationalized this as Servant Leadership,[19] but, between my mirror and me, it was more a form of indentured servitude. A trusted mountaineering guide once told me there comes a point on certain ascents—the crux moment—beyond which the safest way down is up. CAN was my crux moment. Now, there was no turning back.

At this particular time, I had the dual task of raising both debt and equity. Either is a full-time job, but I couldn't afford help and Z was distracted by the possibility that he'd be acqui-hired (the term

---

18   A common instrument used for seed-stage and other early financing rounds.

19   A phrase coined by Robert Greenleaf in his 1970 essay "The Servant as Leader."

for an acquisition made solely for the purpose of hiring the acquired company's team) when another of his seed investments—where he owned a much bigger piece of the pie—completed its sale to a cash-rich competitor. He claimed he wasn't interested in the job, but in the same way your mom tells you she isn't interested in a gift on Mother's Day. Your mom wants a gift, and Z wanted the job. Part of his comfort in spending less time at Dealstruck derived from his confidence in Rudy, his long-time operations lead, who was running the show while I kept marching my boulder skyward on the financing front.

My search for Series A (the first in a sequence of alphabetical financing rounds following Seed)[20] kicked off in earnest at the largest trade show in the industry—Money 20/20. It was early November 2014, and while closing a round by year-end was out of the question, chumming the waters to see which firms were close enough to smell blood wasn't. Though the typical top-tier VC sees more than two thousand pitch decks per year, the majority of what they are being served is frozen fish sticks, not sashimi-grade Bluefin. For most fund managers—venture or otherwise—the hardest part of their job is finding enough good investments, which, for the entrepreneur, means you only have to be a *good enough* investment (I call this investor dyslexia).

So, what is good enough?

I thought Dealstruck might be. We weren't the next Facebook, but we were a real operating business. Each month, twenty-five people (our "complete team") were generating $400k in revenue (our "business model") by originating $4m in new loans (our "product-market fit") across three distinct loan types (our "differentiation").

One of the great mysteries of the universe is why, despite insisting on their portfolio companies being highly differentiated from competitors (code for "unique"), venture investors are themselves

---

20   Startup financings usually start with Seed and then proceed to follow the alphabet. Series A is usually the first round from an institutional investor, such as a venture capital fund. The amount invested often increases with each new letter (Series C > Series B > Series A), as these latter rounds are usually captured by companies as they start to scale rapidly and mature their business models.

remarkably undifferentiated and often travel in packs. Sure, Dealstruck had created some of its own momentum, but what we really had going for us was that fintech was hot and VCs were rushing to make sure they had a "play" in a market that historically attracted less than 5 percent of their investment dollars. This herdlike phenomenon is the VC version of Pascal's Wager[21]: if their play goes bad, that's just startups; if their play goes well, they're a genius; if they don't make a play, their limited partners (i.e. investors) wonder why they are paying "two and twenty" (the typical fee structure for a venture fund)[22]—thus, they always make a play.

It was on account of this financial frenzy that I was able to stack my conference calendar full of back-to-back meetings with investors who were either in fintech or who wanted to be. The only goal of having a meeting at a conference is to set up another meeting *not* at a conference. That high-tech investors embrace such a low-tech solution to sourcing deals would create an existential crisis were it not for their superhuman ability to send texts, check email, and assess the viability of your go-to-market strategy at the same time—a reminder they've figured out how to scale, while you still haven't.

I was preparing for my long roster of meetings when I received a worried call from Rudy: "Hey, we're going to be out of money [for lending] tomorrow. Do you have more coming in?"

There is an old saying that money doesn't grow on trees. But I believe it does. The real problem is that trees don't grow overnight. If you want money, plant your seeds early and often.

As luck would have it, I had sowed a seed seven months prior with a debt fund named Echelon. The plant description on the seed

---

21 Seventeenth-century philosopher Blaise Pascal's argument that a rational person should believe in God. If God exists and we believe, we'll be rewarded; but, if we don't it's off to eternal damnation. If God doesn't exist, it makes no difference what we believe. Since believing in God has no downside, and not believing in God does, we all should believe in God.

22 Investors in a venture capital fund usually pay 2 percent per annum on the assets under management (the total size of the fund) and 20 percent of the profits generated by the fund's investments.

packet said it would blossom in 90 to 120 days, but this particular strain seemed to be late maturing, probably taking its cue from Vik, my baby-faced negotiating counterpart. Vik was the stereotypical twenty-something Wall Streeter who parlayed two years at a big-name firm into a role at a boutique shop where he was given too much responsibility too soon (sound familiar?). As a result, his main negotiating tactic involved deferring to his attorneys, who—like all good hourly billers—were ardent disciples of the Parkinson Principle ("work expands so as to fill the time available for its completion").

Unfortunately for me, the time for completion was now. So, I cancelled all my VC meetings, with no certainty I'd get them back, and hunkered down next to an unencumbered electrical outlet for the remainder of the event. After thirty-six hours chasing down every last item on a closing checklist sufficient to make NASA cringe, Vik sent me a wire confirmation for $1m at 1:46 p.m.—fourteen minutes later our account would have gone negative.

Back home, the wheels kept spinning, although they wouldn't for much longer if I couldn't convince at least one of the VCs that I had just blown off to write me a check in the next ninety days. Along with births, deaths, weddings, and graduations, I'd been told venture meetings are things you absolutely don't miss. But I'd also been told rules one, two, and three of CEO-ing: (1) never run out of money; (2) never run out of money; (3) don't forget rules one and two. To my surprise, the VCs I bailed on interpreted my Money 20/20 fire-drill as proof-positive that I could *do* the job I only would have *told* them I could do had I spent fifteen minutes shooting the shit. By the following week, I had all my meetings rescheduled.

Live demos always beat pitch decks.

Conventional wisdom holds that to get the attention of a top-tier venture firm, you need a piping hot introduction. These guys were using LinkedIn before LinkedIn existed, and if you couldn't navigate to a referral from a trusted connection, how the hell were they to believe you could lead a thinly capitalized, resource-constrained, no-name upstart to the pinnacle of a market filled with highly capitalized, resource-rich, brand-name incumbents? Fortunately, I had an advisor, Cliff, with friends in high places; this despite having raised nearly $150m from these friends without returning hardly any of it. For all its insanity, that he still has friends is one of the few redeeming qualities of the venture ecosystem—subtle acknowledgment of the bad odds facing good people ("it's okay to lose money, as long as you lose it honorably").

The main goal of a warm intro is to find your way immediately to a partner—someone who can make investment decisions. I was told repeatedly by fellow entrepreneurs not to entertain a VC meeting without a partner present. Analysts and associates, they said, are, at best, well-educated gatekeepers, and, at worst, high-class cold-callers trying to hit quota (the unintended consequence here being that twenty-two-year-old first-years are now called partners).

I flew all over the country that December, from partner to partner, except for one blind date on my home turf with a cold-calling associate from Trinity Ventures named Matt, who was tasked with finding his firm's fintech "play." That the market for lending to small and medium-size businesses (SMBs) was huge, hot, and being snapped up daily by its Sand Hill[23] compatriots meant most of my pitching had already been done for me. If what I'd heard about the criteria for early-stage venture investing was true—big markets, great teams—I wouldn't have to do much more than show up with resumes and wire instructions to land the deal.

Though I had generated interest from no less than a dozen firms in the weeks before the holidays, Trinity took pole position right after the New Year. While the skilled CEO tries to create competition, the skilled VC tries to avoid it—they'd been at it twenty-nine years; I'd been at it two. Needless to say, my skills were lacking. I could have slowed them down to try to create a photo-finish (the more people in the picture, the better the valuation), but these guys were one of only two firms that had come off the blocks, and I was

---

23   Sand Hill Road is a famed corridor in Menlo Park that houses many of the world's most prolific venture capital firms.

fearful of a situation where we were long on suitors, short on term sheets, and out of money. In fact, this would have already been the case in the first week of January had I not closed on a $1m bridge loan (an injection of capital designed to last from present-day to a financing milestone close ahead) over the objections of Zalman, who was comfortable driving a loaded 747 full-speed down a short runway instead of borrowing an extra mile to assure takeoff.

The due diligence process was not much of a process at all. While most of the lenders I was negotiating with were giving me a rectal exam, the venture experience was more of a check on the vital signs.

A couple partners from Trinity flew down to "kick the tires," to meet the team and confirm they were indeed about to invest in a living, breathing company with no obvious signs of dysfunction. After meeting with each member of my management team—including Rudy—Noel, the founding partner of Trinity, took me into a room to tell me he wanted to bring the deal to the partnership. Part of his comfort investing in a first-time CEO came from Z's frequent and active involvement in matters of strategy, operations, product development, and personnel. Noel was comfortable investing in me so long as he was also investing in Z—someone who could step in to drive if I steered us off the tracks.

Two weeks after their visit, I flew to Palo Alto to present at Trinity's weekly Partner Meeting. On the flight, I made one last modification to our deck. The final slide—The Ask—originally $5–7m, would now read $10m.

After two years of keeping a capital-intensive business hanging on by a piece of dental floss, I had finally had enough with sensitivity to dilution. It's a cliché but true that most things in business take twice as long and cost twice as much as expected. Our model suggested $5m would get us eighteen months down the road. So, I asked for double. I simply did not have the energy to continue suffering the daily mental anguish that resulted from knowing any one misstep would be our last.

The meeting itself was uneventful. By this point, there weren't questions for which I didn't have answers. Partners could disagree with me, but they couldn't stump me.

After a ten-minute caucus, during which I waited alone in an adjacent conference room, Noel arrived to tell me that the partnership voted 8–1 in favor and that he was ready to issue a term sheet.[24] I wanted to raise $10m; he offered $8m. I wanted a pre-money valuation of $40m;[25] he offered $32m. They say "close enough" only counts in horseshoes and hand-grenades, but I'd add valuation to that list. Why be greedy? I'd probably be in a board room with Noel for the foreseeable future, so I didn't see the point of pushing back on terms that were down-the-middle and fair. Plus, if my other Board members didn't like the deal, one of them could wear the black hat.

It was late January 2015. Having already rejected a $50m private equity term sheet for a controlling stake in the business, we had one term sheet in hand, a few in the bush, and two months to close. Trinity had surged so far ahead of the other prospective investors that most chose to tap out, rather than race through due diligence to present a competing offer. Those that stayed in the mix indicated I was at least two weeks away from a partner meeting and that a mid-thirties valuation was on the high-end of where they might land. A couple more offers would stroke my ego, but wouldn't change our reality.

I was ready to sign. Zalman wasn't.

After a round of benign negotiating, the pre-money had edged up to $34m. Though Z was eager to sell to CAN Capital for a slightly lower price a few months prior—his rationale being that not even the

---

24 Many funds require unanimous consent from the Partners, so I guess I lucked out.

25 Series A valuation for mere mortals, like Dealstruck, follows a very simple formula. VCs want to own a certain percentage of their Series A investments, typically 20–25 percent. Take the amount of money they're investing divided by their target ownership percentage, to get the post-money valuation (your company's imputed worth *after* the financing). Subtract the amount of cash being invested, and you'll arrive at the pre-money valuation (your company's imputed value *before* the financing).

most inane valuation metric could justify such a price—he was now fixated on a number above $40m having found just such a metric: 0.5x-1.0x run-rate annual origination volume (current monthly origination volume multiplied by twelve). Though this metric was devoid of economic underpinning and was a total construct of hindsight—a few recently inked deals happened to fit neatly within its calculus— it was being spread as something resembling science by one of the fintech industry's more respected investors (a sad commentary on science or, more likely, on the industry).

Since we had originated $5m in December, we were, according to the valuation math du jour, worth $30–60m. It was on this basis that Z latched onto a $40m minimum price target. But if you applied the formula to November (one month prior), our range would have been $20–40m; if you applied it to January (one month later) our range would have been $17–35m. Choice of month aside, I think Z knew he was using flawed math; he was far too smart and far too skeptical to mistake venture exuberance for sound arithmetic. Rather, my sense is that he was still self-flagellating after losing the $33m CAN deal—his words, not mine—and only a number meaningfully higher than the acquisition price would be sufficient to quell his dissonance.

Aside from valuation, Z's other hesitation with Trinity (or any Series A investor, for that matter) related to his Sub Debt. With an injection of real equity upon us, Z wanted to ask Trinity for permission to use a portion of the proceeds from our Series A to repay the money he and my father had buried at the bottom of our growing loan portfolio. When I refused to surface this request, he changed tack, demanding either: a) more equity; or b) language in the financing documents affirming his Sub Debt would be paid off the *next* time we raised dough (we hadn't closed Series A and Z was already negotiating Series B). Neither request was reasonable. I cared for Z personally, but I couldn't champion his cause. So, when it came time to vote on Trinity, I wasn't sure if he would champion mine.

I called a Board meeting at our attorney's office to vote on the term sheet. I led with my view: the firm is tier-one; the price is fair; the terms are market; we need the dough; and we have no other options.

What followed were two hours of threats, shouts, curses, and insults hurled back-and-forth between my father, in favor of the term sheet, and Z, against it. I merely ducked for cover. I imagine this would have been a typical dinner conversation had my parents not divorced. By the end of the meeting, the two of them sat exhausted and sweaty, like heavyweight boxers after a twelve-rounder that went the distance. I motioned to approve. Everyone else did the same.

On the day I should have felt my best as an entrepreneur, I felt my worst. I signed the term sheet and walked out.

CHAPTER 10

life
interrupts

WHILE THE SERIES A DRAMA WAS CARRYING ON, I managed to do something that I hadn't done in more than five years: get a date.

That I got a date was only slightly more miraculous than the fact that I actually wanted one. For the better part of my twenties, I described myself as "indifferent" when it came to matters of the opposite sex, though, if you believe in the wisdom of crowds, "incompetent" was more accurate. I wasn't a mutant. I was educated, employed, athletic, capable of holding a conversation, and, if not mildly attractive, at least only mildly unattractive (did I mention humble, too?). But for whatever reason, one thing I wasn't, at least when it came to women, was interested.

I managed to convince myself there was virtue in my indifference, almost to a point of conceit. I told myself I was self-aware ("I'm not ready to be a good boyfriend"). I told myself I was independent ("I'm very happy on my own"). I told myself I was mature ("I'm not looking for a hookup"). And, for the past two-and-some-odd years, I told myself I was an entrepreneur who was too busy daring to be great to indulge in the average Tarzan's trivial needs for physical gratification, emotional nourishment, and psychological support.

I told myself these things until I finally remembered what a fellow entrepreneur once told me—don't defer your life.

My friend Cliff was forty-two years old and fresh off sixteen years as a founder and CEO of two technology startups that were sold, as he put it, "honorably, but not lavishly"—an elegant way of saying what's been said whenever a deal is announced, but its price isn't. For the first time in nearly two decades he didn't have investors to answer to, conferences to speak at, or employees to care for, which left him exposed to an inconvenient truth—he was alone.

Cliff wasn't supposed to end up this way. He was a big believer in prevention being the best cure, and the cure for his loneliness was supposed to be youthful entrepreneurial success—measured in millions of U.S. Dollars—that didn't show up according to plan. His was a worldview where love went only to the highest bidder and he was the low stack at the table. So, he kept taking his medicine, year after year, one financing after another, until his prescription ran out of refills. At this point he had to face the fact that the only love he couldn't afford was his own, and that there is more than a little truth in needing to love yourself before you love someone else.

If your doctor prescribes wealth as the cure for loneliness, I suggest you seek a second opinion.

Unfortunately, I tended to subscribe to a similar ethos governed by a belief that only achievement justified existence. That before I was worthy, I needed net worth. Perhaps this is why I became an entrepreneur—to give myself small odds of a big exit with enough time left to find a partner, meet her parents, and start a family before old age diminished my desire or her ability. Every aspect of my life existed on a single plane, which meant that I could only progress in sequence, not in parallel—first, professional success, then personal success. If the former never came . . . well, I hadn't really considered that.

Which is probably why I went looking for a date at the precise moment when Dealstruck was at its apex and when I was, on paper, a multi-millionaire (though I'd been warned "you're nothing until you sell").

I met Maria through a friend. Sort of.

My sister, two years my senior, had signed me up for a dating app that recommended matches based on mutual connections. She'd found her beau using this service after more than a decade of insisting that men are stupid, marriages are stupid, kids are stupid, and she, being smart, was going to steer clear of it all. Feminism drove her indifference. Entrepreneurship drove mine. We all have our defenses.

At first, I was reluctant to participate. I clung fast to the notion that every good romance had its start in serendipity—that love was a mystical phenomenon, not a statistical one.

Apparently, many people felt this way about founding startups, though I didn't. I remember how frustrated Candace had gotten, trying to catalog my Founder's Story. She was looking for something involving psychic dreams or invisible voices or spontaneous enlightenment, but all I could give her was a sterile analysis of market size, competitive landscape, and unit economics. It turns out many Founders' Stories work this way—a rational, researched, scientific approach to identifying a big opportunity to build a big business is reduced to epiphany.

If we could make ourselves believe in magic after the fact in business, why couldn't we do the same in dating?

I'd come across more than one person who had invoked Excel spreadsheets, regression analysis, and the law of large numbers to generate an optimal dating strategy. That all of these people were still on the market spoke to the effectiveness of their approach (the problem being the algorithms only improve with more observations). But waiting for stars to align, or for mountains to move, or for seas to part wasn't serving me much better, so I gave in to a slightly more scientific approach to partner selection.

During my first few months on the app, I "liked" a few profiles and a few profiles "liked" me back. But I never once messaged any of my matches. This was the "I smoked but I didn't inhale" technique to online dating– a way to get a second-hand high while I wrestled with the fear that actually using would make me an addict. But then I saw Maria and I took my first hit. It would be my only one.

On our first date, Maria greeted me at her door with a big smile and a bigger hug. Wanting to end on a high note, I actually thought about turning around, getting in my car, and driving the hour-and-fifteen minutes from Newport Beach back to San Diego before things got worse. But I fought my better instincts and walked upstairs to her living room overlooking the Pacific.

I had spent hours during the week making plans, backup plans, and backup to my backup plans in an effort to avoid the "So, tell me about yourself" interview that ensues during the typical first date when two people sit across from each other with a beverage in hand, an hour to kill, and nothing else in particular on the agenda. But after a quick tour of the house, Maria offered me a beer, we sat down on the sofa, and she said, "So, tell me about yourself." In dating, as in startups, ideas are a dime-a-dozen—execution is everything—and I hadn't executed my plan. It was 4:30 p.m. and I was on the clock.

Having spent the past two years in a continuous state of pitching, I had become accustomed to reciting my CV in a tight sound bite: son of an entrepreneur, I went to Wharton, worked on Wall Street, and was on the founding team of a successful Internet startup before putting my experience in finance and technology together to launch a disruptive online lender. In the context of seeking capital, I knew the exact things my audience wanted to hear. But in the context of seeking romance, I didn't have a clue. What followed was a rambling twenty minutes that started with my parents' divorce, ended with my business, and meandered through topics such as depression, money, sports and, oh yes, don't forget, prior girlfriends. Nailed it.

I was prepared to show myself the door, but Maria wasn't cruel enough to send me home without dinner. She grabbed a skateboard and I grabbed a beach cruiser, and off to the pier we went.

I don't remember what we talked about. I just remember running out of things to say. In the past, I would have been comfortable allowing for awkward silence. But this time was different. I leaned in for a kiss. She kissed back.

From the first moment I met Maria, I was struck by her unbreakable optimism, her everyday gratitude, and her inner compass—perfectly calibrated to seek joy in life without judgment or reservation. That she happened to be an electrical engineer with a Stanford MBA and a job in private equity made her worldview (quite literally, being that she is from Spain) all the more impressive to me. Peace, love, and happiness were supposed to be the exclusive domain of Yogis, homeopaths, and ski bums. But here was Maria, the exception to my rule.

A couple weeks later, on our second or third date, Maria and I headed to a Mexican restaurant for dinner. I was smack in the middle of trying to simultaneously close a Series A and a $50m credit facility (a type of loan agreement) with just a few payrolls left before cash-zero. All I could talk about were stress, anxiety, and worry. Maria was at a loss. These words simply didn't exist in her vocabulary, and she wasn't keen to introduce them. To her, they were purposeless, egotistic, and self-destructive—the unfortunate side-effects of the American obsession of confusing who you are with what you do.

Maria found my agony that night almost comical. But it was only a matter of perspective. She saw a smart, accomplished, well-educated young man with good health, a loving family, and material comfort lamenting life in a cardboard box under the bridge if his startup failed.

Funny, perhaps, but my fears were real.

In disbelief at what she was hearing, Maria couldn't refrain from double-checking whether I was serious. As we entered the parking lot, she placed her hand on the back of my head and leaned toward me. Chuckling, she asked, "No really, Ethan, what's the worst that happens? You go bankrupt?"

CHAPTER 11

snakebites

AT THE CLOSING DINNER for our Series A, I sat sandwiched between two seventy-year-old men who were rich and success-ful, and who had bet on me to make them even more so. One was my father, Neil. The other was my venture capitalist, Noel. I would have much preferred to be at the "kids" table with the rest of my management team, but finding yourself caught between two fires while your colleagues roast s'mores is one of the perks of being a CEO.

It's standard practice in the venture business not to invest in families given the inherent conflicts between love and money (try firing your wife, then asking her how her day was over dinner that night). This meant that while everyone else in the room was celebrating, my father was mourning—today was his last day as a board member of Dealstruck. Though he knew the venture racket well and though he knew this day would come, it still pained him. I'd like to think his hurt was that of a loving father no longer able to protect his son. But in reality, I think it was that of an accomplished entrepreneur no longer able to be more than a loving father. That his head hurt more than his heart would become apparent when, a few years later, he'd attribute our demise to his absence ("if I were on the Board, things would have been different").

I figured our relationship, at least during Dealstruck, was the pinnacle of dysfunction, but Noel wasn't ready to concede the title. At my dad's probing, Noel revealed to us that he had two sons: one was a billionaire venture capitalist, the other was a regular working guy. He also revealed to us that the quality of his relationship with each was inverse to their wealth. The rich son was arrogant, extravagant, and didn't make time to stay in touch with family (unless he was submitting a competing term sheet). The regular son was the opposite. Noel was unequivocal—he preferred the latter.

The following morning, we convened at the Dealstruck office for our first formal board meeting. I had no procedural knowledge for how to run this startup rite of passage, so I slapped together a few slides of our latest financials and a summary of upcoming initiatives, hoping I hadn't overlooked some embarrassingly obvious deliverable. There wasn't a lot to say that Trinity didn't already know, given the past month of daily communication and closing due diligence. Naïve as I was, I managed to stay on the bull long enough to receive a passing grade at my first rodeo, which in industry jargon is called the Oh Shit meeting. This is a meeting in which the entrepreneur usually reveals some delicate but intentionally sidestepped piece of information right after the wires clear. As in:

> *"Our CTO just resigned."*
> *"Oh, shit." Or,*
> *"Our product doesn't quite work."*
> *"Oh, shit." Or,*
> *"Our burn rate has skyrocketed."*
> *"Oh, shit."*

Though willful deception is wholly unjustifiable, the truth is that even the most pristine startup has warts and it's damn hard to reveal every last one of them while you're walking down the aisle, let alone standing at the altar. That early-stage investors are generally resigned to these entrepreneurial sins of omission is subtle acknowledgment of their complicity in the "Fake it 'til you make it" startup ethos that justifies in the name of Hustle what in any other realm of life might classify as fraud. By the day of your wedding—which is what a venture investment is—you should have sorted out sex, politics, and religion, but whether your future spouse knows your favorite color is unlikely to impact your long-term prospects.

Having exchanged vows without controversy, it was time to celebrate. I did this by spending a few days away; my team did this by spending—or at least trying to. In the wake of our financing, I received a steady flow of requests for more salary, more staff, and more snacks, all of which made running lean more difficult, both literally and figuratively. The ironic part of blasting your financing through a PR megaphone—important for showing customers, competitors, and other investors that you are here to stay—is that after years of trying to hide from your team how little capital you have, you'll find yourself trying to hide from them how much you have.

Back from a short week away, the bulk of my time in the immediate aftermath of our Series A was spent managing relationships with our various lenders. I couldn't have assembled a motlier crew had I tried. Let's meet them:

VINCENT ANTHONY was the Chief Scientist and co-founder of one of the world's largest microchip manufacturers. To me, he resembled a mad scientist—wild hair, long beard, shabby clothes—but my colleagues referred to him simply as The Rabbi (and, they were right, as he would answer more than a couple of my prayers). After nearly forty years of high technology, Vincent had become fascinated by the banal business of lending and was among the fintech industry's earliest, largest, and most sophisticated loan buyers. The night before our first meeting, Vincent sent me a 1,268-word email detailing sixteen specific deficiencies that plagued our budding platform. I would have canceled the meeting had it not been for our mutual acquaintance telling me beforehand that his first exchange with Vincent resulted in the return of an investment memorandum bloody with red ink that also happened to have a $10m check stapled to the back of it. I ended up having a similar experience. Vincent always got to the point, but only after meandering through topics ranging from machine learning to engine mechanics to economic history. He spoke slowly, sought simplicity, and didn't like arm-waving or persuasion—just facts. His deal was supposed to be a simple one—a $5m pool of loans that no one else could touch—though, in the end, I'd put him in a situation so complex that quantum physics could hardly rival it.

BREVET CAPITAL was a small New York hedge fund whose managing partners had financed Z's franchise lending company when they were at Deutsche Bank in the late '90s. Doug, the top dog, had a big mouth, a small attention span, and a constant need to remind people he was really an operator disguised in fund manager form. He wasn't the only one beset by this identity crisis—I often heard lenders claim to have *built* the companies whose assets they merely financed. Brevet branded its capital as "transformative," which is code for "expensive." In exchange for the price, though, they provided size ($50m), flexibility, and, in our specific case, direct access to final decision makers. Having a hotline to the top is pretty important when you're busting covenants, tripping risk-triggers, and beelining straight toward default a few months into a new relationship. Brevet was our most "traditional" credit facility. They loaned us eighty-five cents for every one dollar we loaned our clients, with the difference coming straight from our pocket—in the form of Sub Debt or equity—to absorb losses first.[26] We would end up using every inch of

---

26   Finance company 101 can be described as "borrow wholesale, lend retail." This means companies like Dealstruck borrow from banks or funds like Brevet at, for example, 10 percent and lend to clients at 20 percent. If 5 percent of the loans don't repay, that still leaves Dealstruck 15 percent, of which 10 percent goes to pay its lender and the remaining 5 percent to cover overhead costs and, hopefully, generate a profit. If, however, 12 percent of the loans don't repay, there would not be enough remaining from the 20 percent for Dealstruck to pay its lender 10 percent (20-12 = 8). To protect against this scenario, lenders usually require the finance company to put some money into each loan upfront ("haircut money") that will incur losses first, in case interest on the loans is inadequate to repay the lender. Haircut money is no different than the down payment on a home—it is the finance company version of having equity in the asset it's purchased with borrowed money. To continue the real estate analogy, the amount Dealstruck can borrow on each loan is called an Advance Rate; the home-buying equivalent would be Loan-to-Value.

flexibility we paid for and, to their credit, Brevet always bent without breaking.

BRENDAN ROSS ran a debt fund called Direct Lending Investments (DLI) that burst onto the scene in 2012 to buy high-yield loans from fintech platforms. He was a newcomer to alternative credit, having tired of being the "asshole who fires everyone" as a turnaround CEO. Brendan was a classic case of "kissing up, kicking down" and, as the borrower, I spent the bulk of our relationship stuck between his hoof and the ground. By phone, our conversations bordered on psychological abuse; in person, he couldn't have been more charming. My first conversation with Brendan ended in outright rejection. But when I brought Z to brunch a few months later, Brendan couldn't believe my good fortune—"this guy will make you rich"—and he decided, on the spot, to start buying loans from us. At that time, Brendan didn't know much about asset finance or structured credit, which made business dealings with him like asking a Magic Eight-ball—"cannot predict now" is usually its response. Despite his inexperience, he had the right vision at the right time and, boy, could he sell. During our three years together, DLI grew from $50m in assets under management (AUM) to nearly $800m, with his fees growing proportionally as he'd often remind Z and me along the way. His basic arrangement was to buy loans from upstart small business lending platforms with enough yield to deliver his fund double-digit net annual returns. Though interacting with Brendan wasn't always pleasant, he compensated for it by making deals on handshakes, always honoring his word, and taking risks that no one else would.

COMMUNITY INVESTMENT MANAGEMENT (CIM) was a small "social impact" fund in the Bay Area willing to be convinced that lending to small businesses at 20%+ per annum qualified as a good deed. My contact there—Jacob—was the type of person who must have taken a wrong turn into lending on his way to saving the world. He was smart, personable, worldly, and obsessed with "being a good partner." For a while, I thought CIM was like every other no-name fund I came across that had all the key ingredients lined up except one—money. But I was wrong; they had dough, they simply needed more foreplay before parting with it than the others I'd bedded. After more than a year of getting to know each other, I finally sealed the deal. The CIM facility ($10m) was structured similarly to Brevet, except they provided ninety-five cents for each dollar we loaned and restricted their investment to a single product—term loans. I've learned the hard way that when investors say they are a "good partner" they usually mean they are your partner while things are good. To make money graciously is easy; to lose it that way is much harder. CIM would prove to be a true partner in both good and bad.

Having cash in the bank didn't solve any of our problems, but it gave us time to try. We had no shortage of issues, but most were run-of-the-mill scaling challenges that confront any business preparing for a period of rapid growth: installing more automation; formalizing policies and procedures; acquiring customers profitably en masse; and managing a swelling workforce. These problems don't have easy solutions, but failed iterations only inflict blunt trauma—sure, if you bang your head against the wall enough times you'll end up a vegetable, but an ineffective direct mail campaign isn't a kill-shot.

The one thing that can be fatal in a lending business, especially in the early stages, is making big loans that go bad. Here's why: every time a loan sours (misses payments, files bankruptcy, requires restructuring), you have to replace that loan with cash or another good loan. Even if you have enough dry powder to plug these holes, after a certain amount of deterioration, your lenders can stop lending, which means you stop lending too and, more often than not, you die. This risk—that a small number of big loans takes you down— is called "concentration risk" and avoiding large concentrations is Lesson Two on the Lending 101 syllabus (Lesson One is don't become a lender until you've taken Lending 101).

Even before closing our Series A, Rudy, our VP of Operations, had pressed to increase maximum credit limits (the largest amount any single client could borrow) from $250k to $500k—this in spite of having barely one year of performance history under our belts. His lobbying mainly pertained to accounts receivable credit lines (AR Lines)—that supposed game-changing product he and Z had dreamed up at eCapital—where some of our earliest accounts were outgrowing the current cap. He warned that if no action was taken, these customers would either find a new lender or run out of liquidity before they could (the latter scenario would lose us money and the former wouldn't make us any—not exactly the point of running a finance company; see Ch. 7). "Don't worry," he assured us, "these are good accounts." After months of resisting, I relented. Zalman did, too. And in February 2015, we introduced into our business the one risk we absolutely couldn't take.

Before we knew it, nearly 50 percent of the outstanding balance of our credit line portfolio—approximately $12m—derived from just 20 percent of its constituent accounts.

Making big loans in a small portfolio is like playing Russian Roulette alone—you may not lose, but you'll never win.

There are, however, ways to make larger loans without blowing up.

A little over one year later, Z, sitting in my office lamenting that we went too big, too soon, asked me, "Do you know how you learn to charm a snake?" I shook my head, no. He proceeded:

Step 1: Practice on a slow, non-venomous snake.
Step 2: Practice on a slow, venomous snake.
Step 3: Practice on a fast, non-venomous snake.
Step 4: Practice on a fast, venomous snake. In that order!

Though jumping from Step One straight to Step Four with our AR Line product was a serious mistake, the mere fact we were making some larger loans did not mean they were destined to perform poorly. In fact, up until June, things were relatively docile.

But then we got bit by the snake.

Late one afternoon, Rudy came into my office to tell me we had a problem. A $350k account, ironically named Lo Voltage ("an electrical potential not large enough to cause injury or damage"), had made an urgent request for funding. ASAP funding requests are an inviolable feature of non-prime lending. As such, Lo Voltage's inquiry would have been routine were it not for the fact that they were no longer our customer—at least, they weren't supposed to be. A few months prior, as Lo Voltage ran up against our capacity constraints, we purportedly sold their account to a larger lender capable of servicing their growing needs. Their new lender, however, was refusing to fund and, in dire need of capital, they turned to us as their only hope.

Though I was aware we still had a balance outstanding with this client (while not best practice, it isn't unheard of in receivables finance to get paid off as the invoices securing your loan are collected), I wasn't aware we had already bastardized this account by doing everything we weren't supposed to, and by not doing anything we were.

A quick primer on the AR Line: Consider a small business in need of cash as it waits to receive payments from its customers for a good or service it has already provided. In exchange for immediate cash—usually 85 percent of the invoiced amount—the business agrees to pay interest on the outstanding balance until its customer finally remits payment *directly to us*. We then take what we are due, sending the remainder on to our client. The crux of this whole relationship is the existence and validity of the invoice—which represents a contractual right to receive payment—and our ability to get our hands on the proceeds from it before our client does. There is a whole set of procedures designed to sniff out fraud (e.g., fake invoices), dispute (e.g., incomplete work or defective goods), and misdirection (e.g., customer pays client, not us), ensuring there is money actually owed on the other side of the advance we just made.

Even with these safeguards in place, our business is still a risky one. But there is a right way and a wrong way for things to go bad. The former relates to things outside our control, the latter to things within it. A baseball game should be cancelled because of rain, not because the field crew didn't show up. A car should break an axle because it hit a pothole, not because the mechanic didn't tighten the screws. A fire should start because it's hot and dry outside, not because the cook left the stove on. In lending, there are plenty of right ways for a loan to go wrong: the borrower's business closed; they are in a dispute with a major customer; they mismanaged cash flow; or they decided to run off with the money. But the wrong way for a loan to go wrong is for the lender to simply *let it*.

Lo Voltage went wrong the wrong way.

All that said, one data point doesn't make a trend. So, despite losing sleep over what amounted to our first major loss, I had no reason to suspect any systemic ongoing mismanagement of the portfolio.

But then we got bit again. This time, right after July 4th. Two big AR Lines in one week.

With these two new snake bites, invoices we believed to exist didn't. Now we were owed another $800k and our best recourse for recovery was to channel our inner Goodfella and remind the client they owed us the money *no matter what*. "Fuck you, pay me" seemed like it would be effective as a last resort—after all, wouldn't someone whose livelihood depended on his business do whatever it took to save it? Apparently not. There is a famous quote from J. Paul Getty, "If you owe the bank $100 that's your problem. If you owe the bank $100 million, that's the bank's problem." These clients were our problem and when we came at them with four words of fury, most flipped the bird right back at us.

I remember seeing a former Ampush colleague for dinner that week. When she asked me about things, I told her—only half-jokingly—we were on our way out of business, to which she laughed and encouraged me to stop being my "usual pessimistic self" (I've found in tough times that pessimism and realism converge, and optimism only obscures the truth).

Whatever humor there may have been in my wisecrack evaporated shortly thereafter when the biggest loan on our book—Techwire—turned out to be fraud.

I had been watching this account closely for a few weeks, interrogating Rudy along the way. Had we verified invoices? Yes. Had we validated account debtors? Yes. Did we have recent invoice data? Yes. Were we fully secured? Yes.

Though Rudy's responses indicated he and his team were servicing the account in accordance with proper procedures, both its large balance and abnormal behavior prompted me to dig into the file. Within minutes, I could tell he was lying. Not only was he violating fundamental tenets of lending, but he was aware he was doing so and apparently couldn't stop himself.

Here was a guy who had spent nearly twenty years in commercial finance; who had a decade of experience lending purely against accounts receivable; who had worked with Z twice as an underwriter and senior risk manager; who had built and enforced sound policies and procedures in prior operations; yet, who, at Dealstruck, forgot how to lend.

When I was little, I was a huge baseball fan and I remember marveling at a handful of professionals who, in the middle of illustrious careers, simply forgot how to play the game. Chuck Knoblauch, a Yankee second baseman, couldn't throw to first base. Pitchers Mark Wholers and Rick Ankiel couldn't hit home plate. Greg Zaunn, a catcher, couldn't throw the ball back to the mound. From afar, these stories are humorous. Up close, they are tragic.

Is there any way to see these breakdowns coming? Well, Rudy had dropped me some hints.

Before Techwire, as the first of our King Cobras was inflicting its wounds, Rudy asked me to lunch to discuss, of all topics, stock compensation. He still owned a healthy chunk of the business—nearly 5 percent—but, he was wedded to owning the same amount he was originally granted. Though I had tried explaining multiple times before, Rudy had yet failed to internalize that dilution is like putting on pants—the same for *everyone*. Knowing I wouldn't be able to accommodate his request, I probed from a different angle hoping I might uncover a more creative approach to ameliorate his concerns. I asked, "Let's pretend we're five years down the road and we sell the company. What's a number that makes you happy?"

I expected to hear something in the realm of $3–5m. But no. $100m.

I laughed. But he was serious. And delusional. I told him I'd work on it. He was the most experienced lender in the company (he reminded me regularly) and the thought of him walking out at the time we needed experience more than ever was frightening.

So, of course, a few days later, he cornered me in my office, shut the door behind him, and told me he was resigning. Something about needing a bigger title, a bigger compensation package, and more influence. He wanted to be bigger than the company, and *nobody* was bigger than the company. I'd been told this many times. I knew it to be true. But I didn't act like it.

Instead, I begged, I pleaded, I asked him to reconsider, I told him I'd fight for him. I even gave him some of my own stock. It worked. He stayed. Then came Techwire.

Three months. Five accounts. Two million dollars lost. I had some explaining to do.

CHAPTER 12

no
surprises

I REMEMBER ATTENDING A RECRUITING SEMINAR my junior year at Wharton and rolling my eyes when some bigwig at a bulge bracket investment bank told the audience "our business was built by everyone doing the right thing all the time, but can be destroyed by one person doing the wrong thing one time." Though the impending financial crisis revealed that perhaps the reverse was true—Wall Street had a few more sinners than one at its foundation—the spirit of our protagonist's mild delusion is no lie: success is fragile.

A few short months ago, I had fielded an acquisition offer, raised a high-profile Series A, secured $75m in lending facilities, upgraded my management team, nailed my financial targets, and met my future wife. Now, seemingly overnight, I was hanging on for dear life.

There is a phenomenon common among entrepreneurs and CEOs called Impostor Syndrome with which the afflicted live in constant fear of being exposed as frauds. Where others see skill, we see luck. Where others see competence, we see deceit. Good things happen in spite of us, not because of us. We say we're not worthy. We say we're not deserving. But mostly we say, "if they only knew . . ."

. . . they wouldn't have invested

... they wouldn't have taken the job

... they wouldn't have inked the partnership.

The thing about Impostor Syndrome is that the moment all of the things you are afraid are true actually *become* true, you don't have a syndrome—you're just an impostor. And, that's where I found myself in August 2015 after Rudy started sinking my battleship.

During the fundraising process, Cliff, an advisor whose cautionary tale of loneliness I told earlier, imparted to me his most important rule in dealing with venture investors—"no surprises." When things go wrong—and they will at some point—every fiber of your being will want to withhold bad news, wait until you have an explanation, and see if things resolve themselves. Resist the urge, he advised. Tell them early. Tell them often. There is nothing worse than a surprise.

Heeding Cliff's guidance, I scheduled a trip to Sand Hill Road to visit Trinity and give them the Oh Shit meeting a few months delayed. But before I could tell Noel exactly how deep was the pile of crap we were wading in, I had to ascertain whether our lenders would hand us a pooper scooper or leave us to die like a dog.

The bulk of the problem loans were owned by DLI. To the outside world, DLI was an institutional asset manager, but on the inside it was more of a startup than we were. At the time, the fund employed five or six people arrayed around the CEO's kitchen table. Its risk management systems resided in Excel spreadsheets. Its accounting policies were ill-defined. And its investment process consisted of approval from a committee of one, a secret handshake, and, eventually, a signature on a document whose flimsy verbiage made it resemble a floppy disk circa 1970. That DLI was a new and inexperienced lender run by a somewhat erratic personality had its downsides, but it made one thing certain: our existential crisis would be their existential crisis, too, and when a more formidable lender would have cut bait, Brendan had to keep fishing.

In the face of bad news, Brendan was abusive. But in the face of *really* bad news, he was calm and collaborative. The circumstances we presented him classified as the latter, and a meeting in which I was braced for Armageddon ended with a clean, neat compromise: Dealstruck would repurchase DLI's loans, but cover the losses over time; in exchange, DLI would continue to fund new loans.

With one crisis averted, Z and I headed to Trinity to break early what was now slightly-less-bad news. We still had a $2m hole in the fuselage, but we didn't need to plug it today, and, we could stay in flight while we fixed the airplane. I didn't expect a pat on the back— we'd fucked up big-time and on my watch—but, I did expect someone with more years in early-stage startup investing than I had on this planet to respond to the news with something more than a shocked blank stare. While Noel came to, his young associate, Matt, reinforced our entrepreneurial conditioning by thanking us for raising the issues early, committing to resolve them, and presenting a clear action plan. The problem with "no surprises" is that the need to heed this adage means, by definition, you are delivering a surprise. The best you can hope for is "*less* surprises." But there are times when *any* surprise is too much surprise (like being any dead is too much dead). Though Noel didn't say it, I sensed this was one of those times.

You may be asking yourself how, if I confessed my errors early to my lenders and investors, I was acting as an impostor. The answer lies in my relationship with my team.

Transparency, more than anything, defined the Dealstruck culture and my overriding ethos as a leader. I believe that honesty is the best policy, that grown-ups should be treated as such, and that people who bust their ass to build your dream have a right to know the truth. Being transparent is easy on the way up but, heading the other direction, not so much. After shooting skyward for nearly two years, gravity was now ripping us back to Earth and we were trying to build a parachute on the way down. As hard as it had been to create something from nothing, at least we had started from a standstill. Now, the laws of physics were going to work on our business in a new way and I was getting an unpleasant reminder of Newton's first—turning around takes a lot more force than starting up.

I was tired, I was angry, I was embarrassed, and I was scared. It was fine for me to be miserable—that's part of being a CEO—but, if we were going to reverse course before the ground swallowed us, my team surely couldn't be.

So, I put on a mask.

One thing I always struggled to appreciate was how much my employees inferred from my aesthetic—they were like finely tuned anomaly detection models. The tone of my voice, the length of my gait, the width of my smile (or whether I smiled), the styling of my hair, how firmly I closed my office door, the sincerity of my laugh, and whether I said "good morning" were just a few of the variables running through their daily algorithms that determined precisely how worried (or confident) they should be. When the state of affairs hovers within a narrow band around the norm, these models work in your favor—they facilitate feedback and communication without the need for explicit dialogue. But when tail events[27] occur, particularly bad ones, these models are often hardwired to trigger flight, not fight.

Sure, there are always some startup kamikazes that will fight to the death, but once your business reaches a certain size, people show up because it's a job, not a calling. A little fear motivates, a lot of fear distracts. So I traded in transparency for translucence (and sometimes opacity) in an effort to keep people rowing in the right direction while my inner circle and I feverishly bailed water below deck.

I wasn't the best actor in the world and some days I outright forgot to wear my mask. I felt manipulative. I felt deceptive. I felt dishonest. Staring at my team directly and telling them we had time, money, and answers when in fact we had none of these was among the most difficult and painful feats of self-restraint I exercised at Dealstruck. And, this was simply the beginning. I was living a lie, but I was doing it for them. Uncomfortable as I was, we were still on the top steps of our spiral staircase downward—high ground was within sight—and, thus far, my performance had sufficiently convinced my

---

27   A tail event is defined as a movement more than three standard deviations away from the average (what I've referred to as "the norm"). The term has come to be used less strictly to refer to extremely rare observations or events.

team that regaining it was a matter of when, not if.

Unfortunately, no such recovery was assured.

In lending, we make decisions today, but the quality of those decisions is revealed over time. If I lend you a quarter-million dollars on a three-year term, it could be nearly two years before I learn that wasn't a great idea. If during those two years, before I knew you were a poor risk, I continued making loans to tens of others who looked like you, odds are I'm in for a world of pain. The way to separate the wheat from the chaff with a high degree of certainty is to plant crops, wait to see what's left come harvest time, and adjust accordingly for next season based on the results. This is why lending businesses are best grown slowly (and, historically, not with venture capital). It's also why by the time your portfolio is giving off smoke, there's likely a fire burning below.

Having pushed Rudy aside in favor of leading day-to-day servicing operations myself, this was the reality I confronted. The first five bad AR Lines were the smoke; the subsequent thirty were the fire. With a portfolio nearing 250 credit lines, reporting the exact size of the problem was like trying to provide an accurate casualty count in the immediate aftermath of a terror attack—it took time to sort through piles of debris to determine the full extent of the damage.

In late September, one month after my initial "no surprise" surprise, Noel and Matt visited Dealstruck for our quarterly Board meeting. By this time, the AR Line problem had grown, but I had quantified it, isolated it, and stemmed its expansion. I had also resolved to terminate Rudy and had provided a twenty-page document detailing dozens of operational and technological enhancements in various stages of completion that would prevent any such future crises. Though Rudy's responsibility was to install these policies from the outset, the fact that he didn't was more my failure than his. (In spite of the swashbuckling, shoot-from-the-hip, anti-hierarchical gunslingers we regularly picture startup CEOs to be, there is one management text with a cult-like following among the Valley elite— *High Output Management* by famed Intel CEO Andy Grove. In it, he defines a manager's output as the output of his organization and those he or she indirectly influences.[28] Rudy was part of my organization. That his output was inadequate meant mine was, too.)

But strangely, I was met with applause.

Apparently, the fact I had run toward the carnage, not away from it, was worthy of acknowledgment. We weren't out of the woods, but Trinity finally felt we weren't going deeper into them. With a semblance of credibility restored, I decided to make one last disclosure in the spirit of "no surprises"—for the next seven business days, I would be in Spain meeting my future in-laws, but, fear not, I'd be wired and available.

Never mind that I hadn't spent a full week away in the three years since I started the business. Never mind that without a respite from the past four months of firefighting, my next vacation would be a one-way ticket to a tall bridge. Never mind that I couldn't make or break the company in the course of a few days. Maria would be forever. Dealstruck wouldn't be. Making the trip was an easy decision, right?

Not exactly. My heart knew the correct answer, but my head didn't. And, the mind is exceedingly powerful. Thankfully, Z stepped in to provide me perspective. He wrote:

> As CEO, there's never a good time to take a vacation, and no vacation is ever too short—everyone is always looking for you . . . So, please take the vacation and enjoy it. Be patient when people call you and you have to work, but also turn off the phone, do not open mail all the time, and take the time to see the sights and have fun. Don't work all day while you're there.
>
> Look, the following only happens once in your life: you're 29, walking in the Salamanca district looking for the best tapas in town, beautiful girl holding your arm. What do you do next? No, you don't check email. You squeeze her tight and hold on to the moment, so that you never, never forget it.
>
> And I can assure you that, when you're on your deathbed,

---

28   Andy Grove, *High Output Management*, 2nd ed. (New York: Vintage, 2015).

you will not remember any of the calls, emails (or faxes!), but you
will wish you'd had more of those walks.

He was right. So, off I went. And, on my deathbed, I will remember that trip.

Less than two weeks later, I was back in the saddle, recharged, and ready to ensure we had the resources necessary to execute on our turnaround.

The first task at hand was to part ways with Rudy. Just one problem—he wasn't there. Despite the ninety-day transition plan we had mapped out together, Rudy found my trip to Spain a convenient opportunity to get out of Dodge before it became abundantly clear to others that he'd set the place ablaze. Until this point, both Z and I had attributed Rudy's errors to incompetence, not intent. But his departure raised questions. That someone who Z treated like family for fifteen years wouldn't honor his request for an orderly transition suggested he knew something we didn't. We never uncovered fraud (though he did make undisclosed loans to a family business), but the circumstances surrounding his exit still leave some questions unanswered.

The second task at hand was to promote Steve. Though Steve had been running Credit (deciding who will pay us back) since inception, his experience with Servicing (making sure they do) was decidedly limited. But we were starved for time and money, so in the same way hunger can make a world-class meal out of a Hot Pocket, Steve looked as good to us as hiring JP Morgan himself. To avoid an "up or out" situation—we still wanted Steve to run Credit even if he couldn't handle Servicing—we offered to pay him for ninety days as if he was promoted, but we refused to formalize it with a title change until the trial period was complete. He initially found this arrangement confusing—naturally so, given his military background where title and authority go hand-in-hand—but, he finally understood it was a free option. And, no one turns down a free option.

The third task at hand was to find more money. Given the

circumstances, the only people who *might* reach into their pockets were those already in the deal. To prove to outside investors that our problems were behind us, we needed time to pass without additional setbacks. Exactly how much time we needed to buy was uncertain, but it certainly was more time than we could currently afford. Before I could approach the existing angels with an ask, I had to know if Trinity, our largest and most influential investor, would participate in a bridge round—an important sign of support to others who were more passive and less informed. After three months of regular play-by-play and a vote of confidence at our last Board meeting, I scheduled a late-October visit to Trinity where I'd walk in with my hand out.

In preparing for the meeting—which I would attend alone—Z had serious concerns about how painful the financing terms from Trinity would be (this is like worrying about the cost of stitches while you are bleeding out). We both knew Trinity had all the cards, which meant the only way to exert leverage was to threaten to stop playing the game. So, Z helped me craft a script in which I would suggest politely to Noel that I was willing to take *some* pain, but not an *infinite* amount.

The anticipated terms of the financing didn't worry me. I was already reconciled to the fact that my stock was likely worthless and that the exercise underway was purely one of landing the plane with as little collateral damage as possible—save money, save jobs, save our reputation. I wasn't happy about it, but I understood my obligation to stay the course even when there was no economic rationale for doing so. I was deeply committed to Trinity, my other investors, my lenders, and my team (though, I'm not sure any of them knew it). The only way I was leaving this mess was in victory or in a body bag.

In spite of my better judgment, I sat down across the table from Noel—mano-a-mano—and delivered the message just as Z and I had rehearsed.

I wasn't sure Trinity would participate and, in truth, I wasn't sure I wanted them to. I'd already tried once to dump the CEO role on Z with an honest admission that I was in over my head. If Trinity threw in the towel, I'd have an opening to honorably do the same.

Maybe Noel could tell part of me didn't want to go on.

Maybe Noel thought our problems were beyond what money could solve.

Maybe Noel found it detestable that a first-time CEO who had blown through $8m of his firm's money in a year's time was threatening to quit if the deal wasn't sweet enough.

My guess is the latter. And, I wouldn't blame him. Who's talking sometimes matters more than what's said. What may have been appropriate coming from a gray-haired, fifty-year-old multimillionaire entrepreneur was anything but appropriate coming from me.

Unsurprisingly, Noel indicated he wasn't inclined to provide capital.

I had, according to him, lost credibility as CEO when the size of the AR Line problem grew between our first meeting in August (recall, blank stare) and our second in September (recall, applause). In an effort to adhere to the "no surprises" mantra, I had intentionally delivered bad news early without complete information. Thirty days later, with the ultimate size of the problem understood, Noel confused the fact that I had diagnosed its increase in magnitude for evidence that I had caused it.

This was a classic case of damned if you do, damned if you don't (which, it turns out, is the case with most things in running startups). Had I waited a couple months to provide a single, accurate assessment of the scope of our issue, I would have been chastised for withholding material information from the Board. But by providing multiple, dynamic assessments early, I was classified as incompetent, unaware, untrustworthy, and in my role as messenger I was seen as the root of the problem itself.

There is a concept in quantum physics called Heisenberg's Uncertainty Principle that—in lay terms—states "we cannot measure the position (x) and the momentum (p) of a particle with absolute precision. The more accurately we know one of these values, the less accurately we know the other."[29] I'm no scientist, but I'd say this law of motion governing our infinitesimally small particle friends reveals to us a profound fundamental truth: you can't have it all. Some things in life entail inherent trade-offs, meaning they can't be maximized at the same time. Speed and accuracy are two of those things. The Valley, in general, understands this. It's why catch-phrases like "always be shipping," "done is better than perfect," and Facebook's famous "move fast and break things"[30] are dogma among startup investors and operators alike. It's why "no surprises" is gospel—*any* info sooner is better than *perfect* info later. You can't be quick and be error-free. VCs have opted for the former. Except, in this instance, Noel hadn't.

As I stood outside Trinity's office waiting for my cab to the airport, I called Z and my father together—"Guys," I said, "we'll be lucky if we can sell this for a buck."

No one disagreed.

One week later, I met Z for coffee to discuss the fate of Dealstruck. Even without Trinity, we were committed to finding a soft landing, so I was prepared to put up a "for sale" sign and make some lucky dollar-store shopper the deal of the century. But Z wasn't. Why the change of heart?

Well, he had spoken to Noel, and in regard to funding, Noel was willing to change his mind provided Dealstruck was willing to change its CEO.

Deserving or not, I wasn't surprised or upset. My father always told me there are only two certainties in the life of a CEO: 1) You will never hear thank you; and 2) You will get fired. That Noel felt I was not the person best equipped to dig us out of the mess was

29   Alok Jha, "What is Heisenberg's Uncertainty Principle," *The Guardian*, November 10, 2013, https://www.theguardian.com/science/2013/nov/10/what-is-heisenbergs-uncertainty-principle.

30   Having survived everything they broke to become a $400b+ behemoth, Facebook has since moved to "Move fast with stable infrastructure."

understandable. Why he felt this way was not.

There is a psychological phenomenon called Fundamental Attribution Error that refers to our tendency to attribute an individual's behavior to internal "dispositions and intentions and [discount] the role of the situation as the other perceives it."[31] This bias ignores the other's context and leaves him no room to be a victim of circumstance—every one of his actions reveals an underlying character truth. If someone cuts us off in traffic, he's an asshole, not a caring parent racing to a child's hospital bedside. If someone mistakes our food order, he's an idiot, not a distracted lover who just learned he was dumped. If someone travels to Spain when his company is struggling, he's uncommitted, he lacks judgment, or he just doesn't care. Noel didn't fully allow for my trip to be about recapturing mental health, regaining energy for the turnaround, or honoring the first time I met my life partner's parents.

That his interpretation was far from the truth was evidenced by Z imploring me to stay and imploring Noel to let me. He did. So I did, too.

I'd gotten this far as an entrepreneur on a gas tank full of rejection and doubt—nothing inspires greatness as much as your greatness being in question. Mostly, my detractors remained outside the Dealstruck walls. Now, there was a cynic among us and I wanted nothing more than to prove him wrong.

---

31   Daniel Kahneman and Jonathan Renshon, "Hawkish Biases," in *American Foreign Policy and the Politics of Fear: Threat Inflation Since 9/11*, eds. Trevor Thrall and Jane Cramer (New York: Routledge Press, 2009), 79–96.

bridge to nowhere

EVEN IF TRINITY DECIDED TO PROVIDE US with a small emergency food store, it was time to go on a diet. I had never orchestrated a layoff before. Though I lived through a few rounds of very public cuts at Lehman, they were beyond view internally—it took weeks to realize your daily coffee run had decreased by one. In a large company, impending layoffs are known by all, but the event itself is seen by few. In a small company, they are known by few, but seen by all.

The relationships that make it possible for three people in a garage to obsolesce three thousand people in a skyscraper are best described as co-dependent. Everyone in a startup—the Founders included—knows what they've chosen to pursue isn't rational. Willful self-deception is a prerequisite to voluntarily fight long odds for less pay and more work, stress, and risk. Part of you knows that you're jumping off a bridge and that you probably shouldn't, but, hey, a bunch of others are doing it, too. That others maintain their illusion is central to you maintaining yours, and this mutual need for reciprocal insanity is what ties people together tightly enough to withstand onslaughts from the outside until dream becomes reality. These ties are sometimes referred to as culture—or at least a key component of it. But the interconnectivity that makes startup cultures so strong also renders them particularly susceptible to shock. What one person feels, everyone feels. There is no hiding.

It was late October 2016. We were just over sixty people and we had targeted an amount of cost savings that required reducing that number by ten. On a nominal basis, ten people is nothing—heck, it's practically an insult to layoffs to call it one. But on a relative basis, 20 percent isn't anything to sneeze at.

We'd already taken the first step in planning a layoff—determining how deeply you need to cut. It is an exercise that happens on a spreadsheet, in the abstract, which makes it easy to honor the "when you think you've cut deep enough, cut a little deeper" rule-of-thumb.

The second step in planning a layoff is much harder—and that is to determine *who* you need to cut. Now, you're not talking about overhead ratios or department staffing levels or monthly burn; you're talking about real people with real families who will suffer real consequences without a paycheck. What was, moments earlier, a sterile modeling task suddenly becomes an emotional chore complicated by remorse and regret. "Cut until it hurts" feels sensible in theory, but in practice it feels cruel. Deleting cell C16—Executive Assistant—is different than deleting Sandy in Admin.

Staying committed at this phase of the process is a matter of perspective. There is a famous psychological experiment[32] in which participants, confronted with a morbid scenario, are asked to choose between two courses of action (I've modified the numbers to suit our specific context):

1) If Program A is adopted, 10 people will die

2) If Program B is adopted, there is an 80 percent probability that no one will die and a 20 percent probability that 50 people will die

---

32 Daniel Kahneman and Amos Tversky, "Prospect Theory: An Analysis of Decision Under Risk," *Econometrica* 47, no. 2 (1979): 263–91.

Most people will choose Program B. But if you present the choices slightly differently . . .

1) If Program C is adopted, 40 people will be saved

2) If Program D is adopted, there is an 80 percent probability that 50 people will be saved and a 20 percent probability that no one will be saved

. . . most people will choose Program C.

In our particular circumstance, Program A and Program C are layoffs; Programs B and D are staying the course. Your task—should you choose to accept it—is to choose Program C, so start thinking of it that way.[33]

Now that you've done your planning, there is only one step left: laying people off. Just as building a business on paper is far easier than bringing it to life, deciding who to lay off is far easier than actually handing out the death sentences. This process is like eating hot wings—messy no matter how many napkins you use. With Z's help, we stealthily invited the "cut list" to attend a meeting across the hall where, upon entering the conference room, they would unexpectedly encounter our Director of HR awaiting their arrival. While she and Z broke the bad news, I congregated the rest of the company to discuss the actions presently underway. The moment you say "layoff" you have, at best, 120 seconds before you lose your team's attention, so I planned to emphasize three things:

---

33 The real example is more extreme, which probably results in a stronger display of the Isolation Effect than our example. The choices are between: a) 200 people live, or b) 1/3 chance 600 people live and 2/3 chance no one lives; and c) 400 people die, or d) 1/3 chance no one dies and 2/3 chance 600 people die. Though we replace a 33 percent chance everyone lives with an 80 percent chance everyone lives, the point remains the same: we are unwilling to risk certain life when framed in terms of survival; yet, in direct contradiction, we're willing to do so when framed in terms of death. Though I've demonstrated with probabilities that create identical survival outcomes, the reality is not so rosy: not doing layoffs makes the probabilities more like the reverse— 80 percent chance everyone dies and 20 percent chance 40 people live.

1) The cuts were complete; no additional cuts were
    expected (job security)

2) The cuts were painful (sympathy)

3) The cuts were done to position us for long-term success
    (optimism)

As architect of the layoff, I was trying to avoid the Unintended
Exodus. This occurs when people you hope to retain end up leaving
because they are some combination of scared, bummed, and angry.
Though the Exodus often plays out over the ensuing weeks after a
layoff—it takes time to look for a new job—we luckily avoided any
such desertion this time around.

The immediate aftermath of a layoff is depressing, but that
slump is usually short-lived. For a couple days, productivity may
slow and enthusiasm may wane—it did for us. And, that killed me. I
wanted to whip people up, to demand more output, to remind them
time was wasting—after all, we just did a fucking layoff. But I had
to remember that my mourning process took place during the planning; my team's mourning process had only begun. Healing is not an
instantaneous process, and I've found that if you give people some
time, they're more resilient than you think. So, I bit my tongue and
waited for the inevitable return to normalcy.

Portfolio issues aside, we probably could have avoided a layoff if
we hadn't hired so many people so damn fast in the first place. The
question is whether to hire ahead or to hire behind.

For the better part of two years, we had done the latter. We
squeezed from every one person the output of two, before alleviating
their burden with additional help. Our reasoning was partly financial—we simply didn't have the luxury of adding capacity at the first
sign of strain. But it was also because we simply didn't believe we
had a winning formula yet. In many ways, remaining skeptical of
our own success was healthy—it kept us humble, it kept us hungry,
and it kept our eyes from outgrowing our stomach. It almost broke

us too. By the end of 2014, burnout was rampant. We weren't slowing down, but we weren't staffing up. What kept people grinding was the promise of an organizational chart adjusted for venture financing that I continually assured them was "coming soon."

When it did, people cashed in their IOUs and I made good. That we staffed up quickly didn't mean we hired poorly—it is possible to "hire slow" at the individual level, while "hiring fast" at the company level. But it did mean that, for the first time, we had excess capacity. In the past, growth required people. Now, people required growth.

I'm not sure there is a universal right answer to the hiring conundrum. There are risks to each approach and they can only be evaluated in a case-specific basis. How steep is your growth curve? How deep is your downside? How much capital have you raised and how expensive are your roles (or can you float people until they become profitable)? How is your company being valued (will the market mistake bodies for progress)?

At Dealstruck, though we had a real need for personnel, our hiring spree sprang, in part, from misguided, yet opposing, reactions to venture financing on my behalf—and that of my employees.

For employees, a significant funding round is vindication for choosing startup inanity. But the line between vindication and entitlement is a fine one. The former looks back with a feeling that hard work was worth it. The latter looks ahead with a feeling that hard work shouldn't be so hard anymore—with a feeling I like to call Arrival. Arrival is a dangerous emotion. It replaces skepticism with overconfidence. It replaces humility with arrogance. It replaces hunger with satisfaction. Some of its symptoms are benign—more happy hours, more expense requests, more trashing the competition. But others are less so. Swiss Army knife executives become allergic to grunt work; problems, even small ones, are solved with bodies instead of brains; mundane but critical tasks fall casualty to the big picture; and line-level employees learn a new favorite word—"scale."

There is nothing inherently wrong with focusing on scale—after all, it is an (eventual) necessity for a successful venture investment. But when barkeeps start recommending tech stocks or when strippers start talking option-ARMs,[34] it's a sign things have gone a bit too far. The same goes for your sales assistant talking scale.

If anyone should be thinking about scale, it should be you—the CEO. But not too much. If Arrival is the employee's ill-conceived reaction to VC funding, Departure is the CEO's equally danger-ous counterpart. Departure is characterized by an overwhelming urgency to turn $8m into $80m overnight. Though I've heard plenty of accusations levied against VCs pushing companies to scale prematurely, in my case, Departure was a self-inflicted wound. Trinity, while not perfect, never once pressured us to aban-don caution for growth (in fact, they did the opposite). And, while I never consciously made that trade, Departure made not doing so harder to resist.

Managing the reactions to venture financing was one of the more unique psychological tasks I faced as CEO. I needed to simul-taneously keep my employees' wheels from touching down, while keeping my own wheels on the ground.

Nothing brought this home more clearly than a layoff.

Now that we were carrying a lighter load, Trinity was ready to have an honest conversation about money. To give ourselves a fight-ing chance to find a Series B or a graceful exit, we needed nine to twelve months of runway, which equated to $5m. Noel wasn't eager to participate—his partners had given up on Dealstruck—but, he wanted to be supportive. "Being supportive" is the venture version of a "loss leader" (something on which you probably will lose money knowing that by doing so you'll more than earn it back elsewhere). A reputation for standing by entrepreneurs in distress is one of the only ways outside of check size and price for a venture capitalist to distin-guish its pile of money from its competitors'. Throwing a bone to sour deals keeps the sweet ones coming. So despite his misgivings, Noel jammed through approval for $1.5m on the basis of having "made more money for the firm than anyone else." In a world governed by

34   A complex mortgage product at the root of the 2008 housing crisis.

the precept of unanimous consent, the right Partner can nod people's heads for them when they won't on their own.

The only condition separating our bank account from Trinity's cash was that we first source the remaining $3.5m.

One tactic used commonly in the venture business to dampen the anxiety inherent in making large bets on half-baked ideas is the Buddy System. If this system sounds familiar, it's probably because you employed it years ago in early elementary school when you were in need of a restroom. In case of accident—you got lost, you peed your pants, or you fell into the toilet—your buddy was there with you. Realistically, there wasn't much your fellow six-year-old could do if anything serious occurred other than share in your embarrassment, but at least you were in it together. As with childhood bathroom breaks, so too with venture investing. VCs just don't like to do things alone. This is why seasoned entrepreneurs advise unseasoned ones to fill their financings with multiple investors; the more deep pockets around the table, the better the odds your investors reach into them. Though the Buddy System is a triumph of form over function, the illusion of safety in numbers is an inescapable aspect of the startup investor ethos.

Given that Trinity invested in our Series A solo (shame on me!), it was my job to find them some buddies. My first call was to Vincent—the Merlin-esque marketplace lending guru who'd already used his wizardry twice to keep us alive when I was out of tricks. Though Vincent's personal piggy bank dwarfed the size of Trinity's fund, he was still an angel investor and, after putting more than a few million into Dealstruck's various pockets, I figured he'd be reluctant to double down.

Framing the Bridge Round to Vincent and my other angel investors was a delicate exercise. I had to be transparent about the state of the company—the portfolio challenges, the liquidity constraints, the growth struggles, and the serious possibility of bridging to nowhere. But I also had to offer hope and optimism, and to outline our paths to the Promised Land if we could buy time. You might think that as

Founder and CEO, my risk would be in painting a too-rosy picture. But in fact, my risk was the opposite.

The beat-down I'd taken over the past six months had me pretty convinced that our future was all doom-and-gloom. Yet, in spite of my malaise, the company was doing better. Steve had settled into his role overseeing the Servicing team, morale had rebounded from the layoffs, and we were pacing toward a record month in the early part of December 2015. Things were far from perfect, but Dealstruck was a growing company with solid positioning in a large, under-penetrated market—still fertile ground for venture success. That I was skeptical was beside the point. The investors had a right to the facts and on facts alone, paying $5m to see one more card was not entirely irrational.

Vincent arrived at this conclusion first and made a large commitment to the bridge. The others followed suit. I was surprised by the nonchalance of my investors' reactions to our AR Line gaffe. What I saw as a fatal slip-up, they saw as temporary turbulence—a fundamental fixture of every startup's flight-path to maximum cruising altitude. Perhaps my pessimism was overblown.

One year later, our cash nearly depleted, I'd stumble across a poignant pair of questions while reading a book on the psychology of white-collar crime: "When does a business go from legitimate but unsustainable to being a Ponzi? And should the intentions of the executives matter in making that determination?"[35] I think we'd all agree that when money from new investors is raised under false pretenses expressly to pay off old investors, a Ponzi exists. But what about when a Silicon Valley sweetheart burns through hundreds of millions of dollars on a speculative business model that is unit unprofitable? What about when the promise of a transformative technology can't be turned into more than a promise? After how many millions and how many financing rounds does the well-intentioned entrepreneur have a responsibility to stop?

---

35 Eugene Soltes, *Why They Do It: Inside the Mind of the White-collar Criminal* (New York: Public Affairs, 2016), 274.

The capitalist says, "When the market tells you." Venture investors not only like speculative businesses that depend on miracles; they *only* like those types of businesses. You're the CEO. Your job is never to run out of money. If someone has a pen and a checkbook, and he starts writing without a gun to his head (or misinformation in it), it is not your right to take the money, it is your duty.

However, I say, "When the business tells you." You will always know more than the market about the inner workings of your company. You may be the CEO, your job may be never to run out of money, and you may owe a fiduciary duty to your investors, but if you're out of magic, stop the show. The fact you can find people willing to walk through a door of their own volition doesn't mean you should open it for them.

At the time of our Bridge Round, we hadn't raised hundreds of millions, nor had we pulled the last rabbit out of our hat. The time would come when another round of financing was wrong, but now wasn't it. Raising money was the right thing to do, but it didn't always feel that way.

With the Bridge Round circled, I was heading into the Christmas holiday bruised, but not broken, and in major need of one week without an existential crisis. Wishful thinking.

On the Monday after Christmas, Steve walked into my office unannounced, shutting the door behind him. I was having déjà vu and for good reason. He was resigning. Rather than simply break the news verbally, he handed me a resignation letter airing three pages of grievances to rationalize his departure. All of a sudden, constants of Dealstruck from the day he joined—the startup instability, the unresolved obstacles to scale, the challenges of cross-functional collaboration—were too much for him to bear. I wasn't buying it. People who want to quit, quit. People who want your blessing before they quit generally don't. More often, what they want is to talk. Your job is to figure out what about.

Talking about feelings is the easiest way to resolve them. But most people—especially men—can't do this. It's not that we're unwilling, it's that we don't know how. Turning emotions into words is a skill that requires practice, and there aren't many safe places to train unless you can spare one hour and one-hundred eighty dollars each week at your local shrink. I've had this privilege for twenty years running, and I'm finally beginning to master my own thinking, all for the price of a master's degree. Most people don't have this luxury. Left trying to express something for which they don't have words, they resort to the last alternative—actions. Helping my team members verbalize their feelings resolved more conflict, created more happiness, and generated more camaraderie than any artifice of management science ever could.

Steve was a case in point. He spent three pages saying what only needed three words: "I am scared."

On a personal level, he was worried that we were using his ninety-day trial run as VP of Operations to hire externally. Though he'd never before expressed it, Steve was still nursing an open wound from when the guy whose mess he was now cleaning up (Rudy) was dropped on top of him without consultation. Eighty-three days into his trial run, and lacking a definitive ruling on his promotion, Steve assumed bad intent and opted for "you can't fire me. I quit."

On a company level, he was worried we were a dead man walking. Steve had spent every day during the past three months doing one thing—collecting on defaulted loans. His day bore a striking resemblance to a bread sandwich—bad loan in the morning, bad loan at night, and more bad loans in between. Whatever good was happening in the company was hidden from his sight. Thus, he perceived his daily drudgery to be a microcosm of the broader business, leaving him no choice but to conclude we were on borrowed time.

I didn't have the cure for Steve's underdeveloped emotional vocabulary, but I could have prevented the feelings that fueled his resignation in the first place.

In the earlier days of the company, providing feedback was easy, even without formal channels for doing so. But as our fight for survival intensified, I retreated deeper and deeper into my bunker in more ways than one. I spent more time behind closed doors. I addressed the company sparingly. If they didn't ask, I didn't tell. Mama always said "if you have nothing nice to say, don't say anything." The problem in a culture of transparency is that no news will usually be interpreted as bad news. In an effort to shield my team from the really scary stuff, what scared them most was my silence. When it comes to communicating, "more" or "less" are much better options than "all" or "none." For a moment, I lost control of the narrative. And I almost lost Steve.

After channeling my deepest inner Freud, Steve and I had an agreement in principle that would keep him at Dealstruck. It was New Year's Eve day, the front-end of a long weekend. Some time to relax after a stressful episode was a welcome sight, but it shouldn't have been. The holiday afforded Steve seventy-two hours to recall his doubts, recover his obstinacy, and reconsider his future, any one of which could result in a change of heart. Usually, I'd avoided firing people on Fridays to deprive them a weekend of idle time—anger, alcohol, and advice from ill-informed friends can only end badly for an employer. But I'd never avoided hiring (or, in this case, retaining) people on Fridays for these same reasons. I should have. Whether you're cutting ties or establishing them, do so quickly.

I'm not a religious man, but idle hands do seem to be the devil's workshop. By Monday, Steve had re-resigned. Unfortunately, he wasn't Satan's only victim that weekend.

Upon returning from a hard-earned two-week vacation over the holidays, Russell, my co-founder and CTO, made his way to my office for our weekly one-on-one. With his laptop hugged close to his chest (the engineer's safety blanket), Russell plopped into his seat with a heavy sigh. Before he said a word, I knew. He was done. Something about grad school, biotech, and moving to San Francisco.

I was twenty-four hours from closing our bridge round. My operations leader was gone and my technology leader was about to be. At this juncture, the evaporation of my management team qualified, at least in my mind, as a Material Adverse Event (which loosely translates to a "Big F'ing Problem"). This is the type of development that investors are entitled to know—both legally and ethically—before they write a check. Given that our need for bridge capital was already the result of one Big F'ing Problem—the AR Lines—a second episode would surely crater the raise.

There wasn't much left to do besides beg, so I did. It wasn't a hands-and-knees sort of beg, but had I needed to I would have. This may sound contradictory, since not long before I'd taken the same tack with Rudy only to be reminded that everyone is replaceable. It's true, everyone is replaceable. But simply because someone is *replaceable* doesn't mean he can *be replaced*. Sure, there were other CTOs out there. Sure, there were other Ops guys out there. But they were *out there*. I needed them *in here*. And, no one from *out there* was going to come *in here*. Not right then.

I finally caught a break when Steve committed to stay and when Russell agreed to orchestrate his exit over an extended time period to allow for an orderly CTO transition.

The next day $5m hit our bank account. We had built a bridge to an unknown destination. If we couldn't find someone to meet us on the other side, it would truly be game over.

punched
in the mouth

*"If there's something strange in your neighborhood . . .
if there's something weird and it don't look good, who you
gonna call?"*

Nope, not Ghostbusters. An investment banker.

Between an investment banker and an entrepreneur, it would
be a close call who could better apply lipstick to a pig—but I think
the i-banker would win. Though I'd done a stint on Wall Street, I
never knew exactly what an investment banker did. All I knew was
it involved long hours and lots of PowerPoint, the combination of
which resulted in Picasso-like pitch decks and Hemingway-esque
story lines (in reality, i-bankers help their clients buy / sell / finance /
restructure). Given the complexity of our situation, two things were
certain: first, we needed a skilled makeup artist; second, we needed
a human Rolodex. I was neither, but an investment banker was both.

The idea of hiring an investment banker was not well received
by Noel. In venture circles, the use of an intermediary to raise capital is a sign of weakness. Consider for a moment the irony that an
online matchmaker like AngelList is lauded for connecting startups
to capital, while an offline one is condemned for doing the same. This

perverse mindset permeates the Valley—machine unequivocally trumping man based on form even when the functions are indistinguishable. Philosophical inconsistencies aside, VCs don't like bankers. If you're not hot enough to raise money on your own, you probably aren't raising any—at least not from a venture firm.[36]

As much as I hate to agree with this rule of thumb, it isn't unfounded. Though bankers may blow through town with a "can't miss" opportunity every now and then, when it comes to startups, most often they're selling clunkers to guys who only travel in style.

On the East Coast, these damaged goods are known as "value investments." But on the West Coast, such a concept doesn't exist. If you're the type of person who always buys a fresh bagel for $1.50 when day-olds are half the price, you're probably also the type of person who won't buy a day-old for a nickel. You prefer fresh bagels, you can afford fresh bagels, and you see no reason to risk buying a stale batch just to save a few quarters. Venture capitalists, like you, are bagel snobs. As a result, parading up and down Sand Hill with a "Clearance Sale" sign isn't likely to win you much interest whether you're going solo or with a banker in tow.

All joking aside, Noel had a fair point—a banker does signal weakness. But we *were* weak. So, he relented and we began the process of selecting our salesman (I use "man" because everyone we met was in fact male).

Hiring a banker is a bit like getting an MBA—if you get one from a top school, it can make all the difference; otherwise, it's probably a waste of time and money. Though we wanted a marquee banker, there was no guarantee a marquee banker would want us. Because investment bankers earn the vast majority of their fees upon success, they have little incentive to take on deals they believe are D.O.A. Thus, the audition process was highlighted by mutual skepticism—us checking the bankers for a brain; the bankers checking us for a pulse. The perception of our long-term viability hinged heavily on the issues

---

36   For later-stage capital raises (Series C, D, etc.), bankers are not uncommon, but by that point are those companies really startups?

in our AR Line portfolio and, specifically, on how persuasively we could answer three critical questions: a) Are losses adequately ring-fenced? b) Are financial costs accurately reflected? c) Are operational safeguards fully implemented? The jury was out on whether we'd convince investors, but a few bankers saw signs of life.

We ended up narrowing the field to two distinct candidates. One was an aging industry veteran who had likely sold more finance companies than I had bones in my body. The other was a young up-and-comer who was less experienced, but more plugged into the fintech "revolution."

The old-guard banker was ready to represent us, but only if we selected a specific goal—sell the company or raise capital. The new-school banker offered to try each in parallel.

After analyzing their attributes, drawing out their differences, and studying their respective strengths, our decision ultimately hung on a single question that had nothing to do with either of them:

Did we want to sell?

This was my moment to be strong. To assert that this company needed to be sold as soon as possible at whatever price possible. To acknowledge that I was tired and out of faith. To admit that our experiment was noble, but our execution was flawed, and that it was time to lay our weapons down.

Though Noel and Z expressed a clear preference to continue independently knowing a sale at this stage would return them little, if anything, they put the ball squarely in my court. The question of whether we wanted to sell became whether I wanted to sell.

Unequivocally, the answer was yes. But I said no. Rather, I think I said something along the lines of, "well, umm, err, maybe, I'm not sure, I can see it both ways, so, yeah, let's uh, see if we can explore both."

Why did I do this? What prevented me from giving a clear answer to a clear question for which I had a clear preference?

Ego.

This wasn't the chest-pounding, status-craving, admiration-seeking behavior most of us think of when we hear the word *ego* ("offensive ego"). Rather, this was the avoid weakness, fend off humiliation, and evade discomfort behavior that is less outwardly discernible, but equally pernicious ("defensive ego").

I've borrowed the terms "offensive" and "defensive" ego from a book written by one of my investors—a talented and successful financial services CEO—that he gifted to me as I was winding down the company.[37] In it, he and his executive coach reveal the damning unconscious effects of ego on your leadership ability, decision-making acumen, and ultimate business success. They begin from the premise that we all maintain two sets of self-images: the first depicts how we *want* to be seen ("desired images"); the second depicts how we *don't* want to be seen ("dreaded images"). Not only are our actions subconsciously guided by efforts to sustain the former and avoid the latter, but these images directly relate to our feelings of self-worth, making the consequences for failing to uphold them severe. The result is that we act to protect these images, rather than to further what we know intuitively is true and right, both for ourselves and for our companies (surprisingly, these often overlap).

In my specific case, I dreaded being perceived as a failure, as a quitter, as unable or unwilling to fight the hard fight, as uncommitted and weak. Noel had implied all of these things when he questioned my trip to Spain. I had to prove him wrong, to show him I was the highly competent, endlessly energetic, trustworthy steward of his capital that he originally considered me to be. Noel was my gateway to the venture world—if he didn't believe in my leadership, who else ever would? How could I overcome his doubts by surrendering?

I couldn't. My ego made the decision for me. So instead of focusing exclusively on a sale, we were off-and-running on the Bipolar Express, half the time searching for a partner (i.e. investor) and the other half searching for a parent (i.e. acquirer). This is not a strategy I recommend.

---

37   Brandon Black and Shane Hughes, *Ego Free Leadership: Ending the Unconscious Habits that Hijack Your Business* (Austin: Greenleaf Book Group Press, 2017).

Though our bankers assured us they could steer the right message to the right targets without causing confusion, our market was too tightly connected and too incestuous to police (NDAs being as effective as neighborhood mall cops). Financing rumors are like toothpaste—once out of the tube, they can't be put back in. So, other challenges aside—and there would be plenty—our two-headed monster created one of its own. Upon hearing we wanted to raise money, would-be acquirers questioned whether our team would stay committed as a small part of a large corporation. Upon hearing we wanted to sell, would-be investors questioned whether our team would have the courage to go the distance, rather than run for the first exit on the freeway. Depending on my audience, I told them what they wanted to hear, but when it's your word against the market's, the market usually wins.

Before we could begin our roadshow, we had to build our pitch book. Though we horsed around for longer than we should have debating the nuanced points of semicolons versus commas, the final product was stunning. Sure, the financials section was a wreck and the AR Line explanation was overly simplistic, but we had made the proverbial lemonade and, in doing so, given ourselves the best chance possible to score a good first impression.

We initially focused our fundraising efforts on private equity (PE) firms. Aside from VC's allergies to investment bankers and value bets, our situation was sufficiently complex that only financial services specialists had the slightest hope of grasping it. We certainly weren't the first finance company that needed to recapitalize itself after a portfolio snafu, but we may have been the boldest. Not only were we asking for the ungodly sum of $50m; we were asking for it at the ungodly valuation of $50m. I'm not sure which is the greater embarrassment: writing this now, or asking for it then.

The size of the raise wasn't entirely our decision—to attract the attention of the PE firms we were targeting, our transaction had to be big enough to matter (they can't invest a $5b fund $5m at a time). But the decision on valuation was entirely ours. Though I was firmly in the "whatever we can get" camp, the board's duty is to maximize shareholder value. So, when your banker tells you a $50m pre-money is within the realm of possibility, it's not so easy to convince your largest shareholders (or yourself) that starting at a fraction of that price is a good idea. After all, it never hurts to ask, right?

Wrong!

Ask your boss for a 50 percent raise and you'll probably get nothing. Ask your boss for a 15 percent raise and you'll likely get something—a discussion, at least. If your ask isn't reasonable, it's a sign you can't be reasoned with. By the same logic governments won't negotiate with terrorists, investors won't bother with an out-of-touch entrepreneur; the perception gap is simply too big to close.

Despite my skepticism surrounding our proposed financing terms, we were cautious never to signal a specific asking price prior to securing meetings (or we wouldn't have secured any). Hence, in early March 2016, Z and I headed east for our first round of investor talks.

As usual, Z was more optimistic than I. Underpinning his enthusiasm was the amount of interest we'd already received as evidenced by our ratios of outreach-to-NDA and NDA-to-meeting. In the startup world, measures such as these are known as "vanity metrics"—fundamentally unimportant gauges of business progress that are easily manipulated to show well (e.g. page-views, down-loads, leads). Meetings mean nothing. Investors are paid to take them. It's what they do, how they fill their time. Getting one proba-bly says more about their calendar than their interest level. Though investors purport to disdain pitch decks packed with vanity metrics, some shops track at least one of their own—meeting count. How else can I explain the cold-calls I received for months after shuttering Dealstruck when a simple Google search would have revealed as much? Sure, we landed plenty of meetings, but we needed to hit the jackpot, not a quota.

The meetings themselves were uneventful. Despite my con-cerns, no one leaped across the table to grab me by the necktie when I asked for a $50m pre-money. We had an engaged audience, we fielded thoughtful questions, and we even received a few compliments.

We had a dozen meetings within forty-eight hours and after each one we practiced the same ritual. Z would look at me and say, "That seemed like it went pretty well," to which I would respond, "Seemed okay." Trying to predict the outcome of an investor presentation based on behavior alone was a lot like trying to predict the future using Tarot cards. In the past, Z usually found himself in the role of limiting my speculation—I had a habit of playing out the future before it happened, getting myself all riled up for nothing. Now our roles were reversed. The guessing game was a great way to kill a rush-hour cab ride to JFK, but only time would tell if our meetings had gone well.

One week later, the verdict was in—they had not.

Mike Tyson, former heavyweight boxing champion of the world, once said, "Everybody has a plan until they get punched in the mouth." Painful as it was, the silver lining of a bloody lip after Round One was the Board finally realizing that simply surviving eleven more was the best we could hope for. Conceding on purchase price, valuation, and the size of our raise didn't guarantee a positive outcome, but it made it more comfortable to search for one.

Though we'd thus far come up empty, the outward signs of progress—travel, conference calls, and data room prep—were sufficient to assure my team the process was going fine. Between trips, I'd get the usual questions from the usual suspects, but nothing that couldn't be deflected by a funny story or a market insight gleaned from my latest adventure. After a couple more months, a few of my savvier colleagues—noticing our sparse investor attendance record—asked me, "Why hasn't anyone come on site yet?" To which I reflexively offered the classic rebuttal, "These things always take longer than you think." Notwithstanding these casual inquiries, the truth is most people were too busy giving their all to make Dealstruck succeed to pay attention to my day-to-day events, let alone the industry's.

But on May 9, 2016, that changed. There it was on the front page of the *Wall Street Journal* in big bold letters, the headline our industry had so far avoided: "LendingClub CEO Fired Over Faulty Loans." The *New York Times* added fuel to the fire: "Avant Cuts Jobs Amid Online Lending Industry's Struggles," and *Financial Times* came at it from another direction: "Prosper Lays Off 28% of its Workforce and Closes Salt Lake City Office." Suddenly online lending was in very public distress.

Headline risk is a scary thing, especially in an emerging industry built on trust. When investors finance or purchase loans, they do so in reliance on a set of statements from the originator—known as representations and warranties (collectively, "reps")—about what will be true, accurate, and complete upon the funding of every single loan. At a high level, reps are simply assurances from the originator that it won't knowingly do anything it isn't supposed to do and that, if it does, the financier will have remedies to rectify the wrongs. Breaching reps is like counting strokes in golf—a 300-yard drive counts the same as a two-foot putt.

In the case of LendingClub, the poster-child of our industry, nearly $1b of its stock market value (35%) disintegrated overnight because the dates on $3m of loans—0.10% of its *quarterly* origination volume—were altered to make it appear as if some arcane clause in its revised loan agreement was disclosed to customers, when in fact it wasn't. Until investors could determine whether the LendingClub fiasco was an isolated incident or an industrywide infection, they decided in unison to step on the brakes. Funding evaporated. Origination slowed. Layoffs ensued.

We had made a habit of holding quarterly management meetings offsite to improve our team dynamics, discuss strategic priorities, and plan for the coming months. At one of our earliest events—in late 2014—Z posed a question to the team, "What is your number one concern regarding our ability to achieve success?"

Most people, myself included, responded with fears about *internal* issues—our credit box won't be right, our acquisition costs will be too high, our processes won't be adequately automated. Z presciently responded with an *external* issue—that something bad would happen in our industry and everyone would suffer. Though I knew well that good luck and startup success went hand-in-hand, Z's cautionary conjecture was a frustrating reminder that our greatest obstacle could be one outside of our control; that even if we did everything right, we could still lose. Z had seen this movie before, multiple times. The Russian bond crisis in 1998 forced his franchise finance company to sell, and irrational competition eliminated margins in his freight factoring business. He didn't think it would happen, but he knew it could happen—and if it did, it would be severe. As my dad, an avid sailboat racer, says, "The wind *always* shifts."

Unfortunately, when the wind shifts against you, not even perfect sailing will get you first across the line. And, even if it could, by now you know we'd been less than stellar yachtsmen. Prior to the LendingClub news, I figured the AR Lines would be the sole cause if our financing effort failed—we'd only have ourselves to blame. Now, I wasn't so sure.

Luckily for me, on the day of the LendingClub announcement, I was in the perfect position to test my hypothesis: an investor pitch. Now, this wasn't your ordinary pitch. I was a couple meetings in with an LA-based venture fund affiliated closely enough with a Big Three consulting firm to require as part of their investment process its stamp of approval. Around the same time that the fund was deciding whether to advance into deeper due diligence with Dealstruck, its partner firm's entire Global Financial Services practice arrived in Southern California for its annual summit. I was asked to present to its dozen partners.

(A moment on consultants, courtesy of my ego: If the entrepreneur's relationship to venture capitalists can be described as love-hate, his relationship to consultants can be described as hate-hate. Okay, that's a little strong. But it is hard to open yourself up to abuse in front of a constituency most of whom have never operated, never written a check, and never suffered any real consequences for the ultimate effectiveness of their advice.)

I stood at the front of the room, introduced myself and my company, and said, "We're an online lender to small businesses." When everyone laughs and you haven't told a joke, you *are* the joke.

I muddled my way through a presentation during which half the room checked email, half the room took a water break, and one particularly ornery attendee medicated whatever unreconciled personal or professional traumas he had by treating me to a historical discourse on how finance companies will all inevitably fail. Period. Paragraph.

To add insult to injury, this particular individual decided to conduct a scientific survey to present me with further evidence of how fucked I was. He stood up and asked everyone in the room, "Raise your hand if you'd take $10,000 out of your own pocket to invest in Dealstruck."

Not a single hand went up.

For as much antipathy as I was feeling, these consultants probably weren't as full of shit as my ego made them out to be. If they bowed out during a presentation in which I only shared the good stuff, I'm not sure I'd even have a chance to reveal the bad stuff before everyone else did the same. Our only hope, it seemed, was that the wind might shift again, this time in our favor. But we had to find a way to keep sailing until it did.

musical
lenders

THERE IS ONE REDEEMING QUALITY to being in extremis—
focus. In the normal course of running a startup, you'll find
yourself balancing too many priorities, juggling too many balls, and
trying to solve too many complex problems all at once. Even when
you are aware that you're over-committed, pulling back is hard. It's
why Steve Jobs is almost more revered in startup circles for positing,
"Focus is about saying 'No'" than he is for any work of technical or
aesthetic godliness he produced. Through some combination of arrogance, anxiety, and incentives, entrepreneurs tend to believe that
they not only can boil the ocean, but that they should. Quieting your
mind and narrowing your field of vision is a conscious act—strong
advisors and directors can help—but, with seemingly endless obstacles to overcome, who has time to be conscious?

For better or worse, this all changes the day you are staring at
a sunset that could be your last. Shipping new technology features,
launching new marketing initiatives, and resolving internal squab-
bles simply won't matter unless you can do one thing—stay alive.

I'm not a big fan of comparing professional crises to truly existential ones. Not to sound cavalier, but as the CEO of a venture-backed
startup there is only one thing at risk—money. Sure, if you end up

with less money than you started there will be some undesirable side-effects to your reputation, your employees' well-being, and your psyche, but those are all solvable. The only thing truly gone forever is money. Building a business—or saving one—is not nearly as heroic as we think. You're not in a war zone or suffering abject poverty or facing personal tragedy. There is no actual *life* on the line, not even yours.

The problem is, in the moment, it doesn't feel this way, no matter what stage of Zen Enlightenment you've reached. That's why as I recount these events—months removed from our unraveling, my own heartbeat tangible proof that The End is not the end—I'm failing in my quest to find any metaphor more apt than life and death.

So, let's pretend entrepreneurship really is a struggle to survive. There are two ways to confront it—the first is to fear death, the second is to embrace it.

I'm reminded of my freshman-year management class—the one everyone thinks is gushy mushy BS, but later turns out to be the most important course we took—where we looked to inspirational stories of survival for leadership lessons. One such story was that of Nando Parrado and twenty-seven of his peers who ended up trapped in the Andean wilderness for seventy-two days after a plane crash. While our professor missed the most important message from Nando's struggle to survive—instead focusing us on what debating the relative merits of flashlights versus signal flares could teach us about group dynamics—an excerpt from his memoir, *Miracle in the Andes*,[38] captures it poignantly:

> *I would live as if I were dead already. With nothing to lose, nothing could surprise me, nothing could stop me from fighting; my fears would not block me from following my instincts, and no risk would be too great.*[39]

---

38 In my course, we read from a different memoir of the same event, but I can't recall the exact one. The themes are the same regardless.

39 Nando Parrado, *Miracle in the Andes: 72 Days on the Mountain and My Long Trek Home* (London: The Orion Publishing Group, 2006), 112.

To fear death or to embrace it? With fear, death is a tragedy. Once death is embraced, life is a miracle. With fear, every step carries the weight of mortality. With the embrace of death, every step offers the opportunity for rebirth. With fear, the mind is your enemy. Embracing death, the mind is your friend. Fear is scarcity—I'm not enough, my company isn't enough. Once you've embraced death you gain abundance—we've come a long way, let's try to go further.

Some people say fear is an effective motivator. I used to be one of them. So, I let it rule me.

Perhaps fear is what kept me moving, kept me searching, kept me fighting. No, I would have done that anyway—relentlessness is part of an entrepreneur's DNA. More likely, fear is what kept me anxious, kept me depressed, kept me embarrassed, kept me ashamed, and, I'm quite certain, kept me from being my best when I absolutely needed to be. Who knows if a shift in mindset would have altered the company's reality, but it would have altered mine and that couldn't have hurt. What I didn't realize at the time was that fear was a choice. The struggles in entrepreneurship are hard enough, and I chose to make mine harder. When your time comes, will you?

Enough philosophizing.

If it wasn't before, one thing became crystal clear on the heels of the LendingClub news—risk was off. In my experience, investors fall out of love a lot quicker than they fall into it. It's hard to get fired for not doing a deal, but it's easy to get fired if you do the wrong one, especially if you do the wrong one at the wrong time. Over the three years that fintech crescendoed, debt and equity investors had been handing online lending startups term sheets like they were going out of style. Then one day the boss went back to wearing a suit and tie instead of blue jeans and a blazer, and everyone got the memo.

Though the broader market was taking risk off, we had a set of lenders stuck with risk they already had taken on.

You may be wondering how, through all of this chaos, we were able to continue funding new loans. Under normal circumstances, a finance company facing our level of distress would have been cut off by its lenders. But as you know by now, our circumstances were far from normal.

Brendan Ross, President of Direct Lending Investments (DLI), was the main reason why.

Brendan had stumbled upon the marketplace lending opportunity early in its life-cycle and had taken a no-holds-barred approach to amassing nearly $1b of AUM in a few short years. An outgrowth of this strategy was that DLI, especially in its early days, was striking deals that were, by traditional standards, somewhere between aggressive and very aggressive. One manifestation of this was Brendan providing his origination partners (like us) with 100 cents on the dollar for every loan funded when most other lenders only offered 80 to 90 cents. Under both constructs we were, in theory, supposed to cough up cash when a loan soured, but where other lenders had built-in protection (the other 10–20 cents) in case we didn't, DLI gave us the benefit of the doubt.

As our coffers dwindled toward late 2015, we had stopped funding with our other main lender—Brevet—to avoid using precious remaining cash on the 15 cents upfront "haircut money." This meant we were in a place no finance company likes to be—wholly reliant on a single funding source. Though we had effectively placed the fate of our company into Brendan's hands, the structure of our deal with him meant that if he didn't keep funding loans, neither would we. And if we didn't keep funding loans, we wouldn't be using any remaining cash to plug his loan losses (see Ch. 11).

There is a saying in lending that "your first loss is your best loss," which is a close relative of "don't throw good money after bad." If someone you gave money to can't pay it back, the usual best course of action is *not* to give that person more money (I believe this falls under "giving crack to a crack addict"). In nearly every circumstance I've encountered with a troubled borrower its "Mo' Money, Mo' Problems."

Taking your first loss is easy the second time, but the first time you're faced with pulling the plug on your money and your client's livelihood, you'll probably end up paying for life support instead. I did. We humans don't like to lose money; in fact, we don't like to lose much of anything—a psychological phenomenon known as "loss aversion."[40] In seeking to avoid loss, we'll do things that, absent the *feelings* associated with pending or actual loss, appear absolutely comical. We'll stay in relationships we know we should exit, we'll pay for options we know we'll never need, and we'll give $50k to a business that already owes us $300k if it means we can push the pain out to a future date. In our effort to avoid losses, we fall prey to another bias—known as confirmation—where we acknowledge data that support our desired outcome and discard data that don't. So, the first time one of my clients sent a turnaround plan that showed how another $50k would dig them out of their mess, I found a way to believe it. A few weeks later, when they asked for fifty more, thankfully, I didn't.

In Dealstruck, Brendan was running up against his first opportunity to take his first loss, and he was willing to fight tooth-and-nail not to. He was managing money for 1,000+ rich people who could ask for it back on short notice and who, he feared, would run for higher ground at even the slightest sign of trouble. If Dealstruck went down, his fund might go down with it. Buying more loans was buying more time, and, to Brendan, pushing potential losses as far into the future as he could—even if they ended up larger—was sound business, not psychological dysfunction.

With destruction mutually assured, we had good reason to believe our loan funding was secure. But on our hierarchy of needs, debt was second; our first was equity, the source of our operating cash, and we were running out. The market was turned off and our existing investors were tapped out, but there was one heavily encumbered pile of cash that we might be able to get hold of. In the process of funding the "haircut" into their credit facility, Brevet had amassed over $3m of cash reserves—extra insurance in case what was happening happened. This haircut had been funded by our Sub

---

40   Daniel Kahneman and Amos Tversky, "Choices, Values, and Frames," *American Psychologist* 39, no. 4 (1984): 341–350.

Debt investors who, at this point, had borne the brunt of loan losses sufficient to endanger their return of principal. Accessing this $3m was our only hope and doing so required a delicate Three Step:

STEP 1:   Convince DLI to pay off Brevet

STEP 2:   Convince Brevet to accept a payoff

STEP 3:   Convince Sub Debt to release excess cash for operational use

Before we approached DLI on Step 1, there had been a Step 0 in which we contacted Brevet about the idea of them "buying" the company. We weren't sure DLI would have the stomach to double-down yet again by paying them off and the prospect of a soft landing with Brevet for the team and the operation—even if it meant a hard landing for our investors and other lenders—seemed as good an outcome as any at this stage. Having long fancied itself a "finance company in fund form," Brevet took keenly to this idea and, for a few weeks, a marriage looked likely. That was, until we met our would-be father-in-law, Rob Leeds.

Rob was the worst of what Wall Street has to offer—arrogant, condescending, and overconfident. He was the sort of person who prefaced most statements with, "I'm not trying to be an asshole, but ...," which only meant he didn't need to try to be one. Rob was new to Brevet—brought in, it seemed, specifically to be the "bad cop" in a working relationship that had been, on the back of Z's fifteen-year history with the fund, cordial to this point. After a few meetings in which he demonstrated modest self-restraint on account of his newness, he made clear a vision for Brevet-Dealstruck that would never work and, on the off chance it did, would not be one that our team would ever work for. It was at this point we flipped the script—"Guys, it's been grand, but how about we just pay you off?"

In doing this, our first step—convincing DLI to pay off Brevet—was easy; they'd pay any price to keep turning over cards. But our second one—convincing Brevet to accept it—wasn't.

There is a variation of the Golden Rule[41] that goes like this: "He who has the gold makes the rules." One rule that Brevet had put in place required us to pay a $1.5m fee if we paid back its loan prior to maturity. This type of rule is not uncommon—after exerting the effort to put their money "to work" (earning interest), lenders prefer for it to stay steadily employed. In our circumstance, however, it was sufficiently punitive to render useless any attempt to access the trapped cash. To make our game of musical lenders economical, we needed Brevet to waive or reduce their fee, and the carrot we were offering was a first-class ticket on the next train out of town when an impending shit-storm was on the horizon. They didn't bite. They insisted they wanted to buy. Entrepreneurial dreams die hard.

It was now the end of May 2016. If I didn't have money by the end of June, I was prepared to walk in on Friday, July 1st and stop the music.

But just when our future appeared hopeless, TAB Bank showed up.

Like Brevet, TAB Bank was small, unknown, and afflicted with an identity crisis: "we're a finance company in bank form," they insisted (can't we all just accept ourselves?). After ignoring overtures from our first investment banker three months prior, one phone call from a more trusted source landed their CEO and key management in our office seventy-two hours later, ready to make a deal. TAB loved our technology, our team, and our brand. They'd been told we were on the ropes, but they were about to find out we were well into our ten-count. Toward the end of the meeting, Curt, TAB's CEO, asked me for an update on our situation.

I was straight: "In thirty days, I'm shutting everything down unless I have a term sheet. My main goal is to protect my senior lenders and my Sub Debt. The terms don't have to be pretty, but they have to be real."

Curt nodded, indicating he understood, and committed to move quickly.

---

41 "So in everything, do to others what you would have them do to you, for this sums up the Law and the Prophets." Matthew 7:12 NIV.

With a savior in sight, we turned back to Brevet. Though their interest in Dealstruck brought them further down the base path toward owning an operating company than they'd ever been before, some deep soul-searching led them to conclude that their all-weather gear would be inadequate to withstand a potential downpour. Finally, they relented. They reduced their exit fee to $500k—not ideal, but still a benevolent gesture—and DLI readied its wire.

The only thing left to solve for was Step Three—convincing the Sub Debt lenders that the highest and best use of the excess cash was to float the company to a sale with TAB (which would return most of their money over time). In theory, this cash was theirs. But they were caught in a Catch-22. If they didn't release the cash for operational use (payroll, rent, etc.), DLI wouldn't pay off Brevet. If DLI didn't pay off Brevet, the cash would be absorbed by Brevet to cover fees and expenses as it unwound its portfolio. Like Schrödinger's cat, the Sub Debt's cash simultaneously did and did not exist. TAB wasn't a certainty, but it was their best bet. My job was to convince them of that.

Calling thirty-one individual investors who had made a secured loan to inform them the best I could offer was a coin-flip they'd get their money back if, and only if, they converted it to equity was an instructive, if unpleasant, experience. The reactions fell into two camps.

The first camp was comprised of entrepreneurs, founders, and CEOs who had amassed wealth non-linearly over a lifetime of owning some or all of the companies they operated. Most had achieved great success after at least one failure and, thus, understood firsthand that death is part of life—especially an entrepreneurial one. Upset as they were with the situation, they weren't upset with me. In fact, they expressed gratitude that I hadn't jumped ship when it was economically rational to do so, that I would commit myself to anything if it meant recovering their capital.

The second camp was comprised of doctors, accountants, and lawyers who had amassed wealth linearly over a lifetime of billable hours and steady paychecks. Most had never taken great risks professionally and, thus, had never experienced great failure. Upset as they were with the situation, they were more upset with *me*. The majority slung insults gracefully, but more than a handful dished out the type of abuse common among angry sports fans who—after a few too many beers—have lost their capacity for words exceeding four letters and are thoroughly convinced their team lost solely to spite them. People seeing this shade of red tend to repeat themselves. The first repetition of outrage warrants an apology. But the second and third don't. Taking their punches with stoicism will give them more satisfaction than your words ever could.

Despite the intensity of their animosity, I was offering the Sub Debt something anger wouldn't—hope. Begrudgingly, everyone eventually arrived at the same conclusion: release the cash and go all-in on TAB.

After chasing down signatures, DLI paid off Brevet, the Sub Debt released the excess cash, and Dealstruck picked up a few months of oxygen to get the TAB deal done.

One problem.

Less than a week after getting all our lenders on the same page, Curt called—the deal was off.

I felt like I was back in middle-school when—in the course of a single school-bus ride—a girl could hate you, love you, and hate you again without you saying a word.

Without TAB we were dead.

Z and I had long disagreed on desperation as a negotiating strategy. Even as we came under severe duress, there was always an element of "playing hard to get" in his approach that I thought worked well when we had time to find a date, but not when we were partner-less two hours before prom. Whether pride or economics drove his behavior, I wasn't sure. But I was sure when it came time to make our last impassioned plea for asylum, I wanted to be in the room alone. Thankfully, when Curt called, I was.

"Curt," I said, "if you don't bid for this company now, it won't be here in thirty days when you change your mind again. Put something on paper—anything—and I will get it done."

He grumbled about due diligence expenses. "Send me the bill," I told him.

"Okay," he said, "I'll keep my team on it this weekend and see if we can make the numbers work."

Between being on the road with our investment bankers, restructuring our balance sheet, and wooing TAB Bank, almost six months had passed since I'd spent any meaningful time on the business itself. That responsibility had been handed over to my number two, Robert Riedl.

Robert joined Dealstruck in May 2015, six weeks before Rudygate ensued (after one month on the job he'd warned me "something's not right with that guy"). We met through a mutual industry acquaintance at a time when Robert was looking for a change after twelve years CFO-ing a public specialty lender and fifteen years investment banking before that. He'd say he was drawn to Dealstruck by our market and by me, but I think the biggest selling point was that leaving his old firm would release his golden handcuffs—a few million bucks of otherwise liquid stock that, so long as he wanted to keep his job, was anything but.

Robert quickly became my most trusted confidante. Here was a guy who had taken a big pay cut for a job with no title, a seventy-five-minute commute, and a set of daily responsibilities more fit for an entry-level analyst than a seasoned executive—all without complaining once. He was steadfastly company-first, his work-ethic was maniacal, and he was fearless.

Though he was an "insider," the fact he hadn't vested any stock, hadn't loaned us any money, and wouldn't miss a meal if Dealstruck disappeared meant he could provide an "outsider's" perspective. Having been around specialty finance for more than twenty-five years, Robert had seen plenty of "next big ideas" come and go, and had a healthy skepticism for anything other than the way lending had been done since the Dark Ages. Venture startups tend to eschew these types of traditionalists as grumpy dinosaurs too intentionally old-school to trade-in their notebook and pen for an iPad. These team members will tell you you're growing too fast, your assumptions are too rosy, you're too reliant on automation, and your "workflow efficiencies" are ill-advised shortcuts. That's not the attitude that inspires entrepreneurs or their acolytes on a world-changing mission. But it is exactly the counterbalance every team needs. I only wish I had hired Robert sooner.

As the TAB deal unfolded, I was pretty sure the *best* outcome we could hope for was one that would make DLI whole and our Sub Debt close to whole, but that, under any construct, would wipe out our equity. Given that my Board members' money resided in parts of the capital stack with no reasonable expectation of return, lobbying them for the TAB deal wasn't going to be easy, even if it was the only option. So, before I started beating my "sell at any price" drum, I ran my reasoning through one final reality check.

Robert agreed. "Any deal with TAB," he said, "would be a *great* outcome."

I was decided. If TAB sent us a term sheet, I wouldn't so much as open the attachment before telling the Board that if they wanted to find a different deal, they'd need to find a different CEO.

A couple weeks later, a term sheet arrived. Like a parent admiring his newborn, I considered it the prettiest damn thing in the world, no matter how objectively ugly it was. And, to Z and Noel, it was very ugly.

None of this should have been a surprise.

In the lead-up to the TAB offer, I had gently guided Noel's expectations toward something close to what we received and Z, depressed as he was, had been involved directly in the negotiations. They had both reluctantly indicated that if we found ourselves out of time and out of options they would push the button, no matter the price. Here we were. Out of time and out of options. But when it came time to act, neither lifted a finger.

CHAPTER 16

the
slow yes

IN THREE YEARS LENDING to small businesses, the number one complaint we heard was not that our prices were too high or that our terms were too onerous or that our criteria were too stringent— it was that our decisions were too slow. Never mind we were doing in three days what a bank did in three months, and we were doing it with less information; the reality was our clients were too busy mowing lawns, cleaning office buildings, or baking bread to be bothered with what they saw as a trivial and tangential task—financing. While we requested more documents, conducted more calls, and analyzed more data to exhaust every angle of a deal before saying no—we called this customer service—Joe Sandblaster wished we'd drop it already and tell him to buzz off. He wanted an answer, any answer, and a "fast no" was better than a "slow yes."

Earlier in our lifecycle, when our PR machine was running full-steam, I wrote a blog post titled, "Your Lender has a Lender Too," seeking to strike a "you and I aren't so different" tone with our prospective clients who were automatically suspicious of the asymmetric power dynamics inherent in the creditor-debtor relationship. We were the big, bad lender; they were the weak, defenseless borrower. We were the screwdriver; they were the screw. What they didn't know was that they were seeing only one side of the equation and that, on the other side, we too were on the sharp-end of a firmly gripped Phillips-head. I wanted our clients to know we "felt their pain" and to convince them our willingness to say so should be reason enough for them to choose us and not the other guy. This isn't the type of macho power-sales technique that makes for a Hollywood business thriller, but I'm yet to find any more reliable method of getting someone to do things my way than by first seeing things their way.

Empathy wasn't solely a marketing gimmick. It was real. That our clients perceived us as more resourced, more successful, and more powerful than they were when the opposite was true was one of the grand ironies of serving small businesses. We simply weren't as different from our customers as a *Techcrunch* article and a fancy website made them think. Nowhere was this more clearly on display than in our mutual disdain for the distraction of fundraising and our wholehearted agreement that a too-early no was superior to a too-late yes.

Getting people to act on your schedule is no easy feat, even when it's in their own best interest to do so. Between the time when TAB gave us a verbal term sheet and when they actually wrote a term sheet, we had completed a debt restructuring that netted us enough runway to make things that seemed urgent yesterday seem slightly less urgent today. Though I had planned for total acquiescence from a Board facing certain death, neither Noel nor Zalman feared the reaper now that our drop-dead date was out of sight. Re-running a financing process when an extra six months shows up is like a terminally ill patient starting retirement planning the day he outlives the doctor's prognosis. Maybe he'll have a long, prosperous life, but planning for it probably isn't the best use of his remaining time and resources.

Because most investors are used to competing to win deals, they tend to hold fast to the unfounded belief that where there is one interested party, there will be many. After nine months of first trying to sell the company and then trying to give it away, I had ginned up exactly one taker—TAB Bank. Though I was convinced I had chased down and been rejected by every other possible acquirer and investor, Noel wasn't. He lived in a world where no one wanted to be the first to move, but where everyone wanted to be the second. Now that we'd found one party willing to take the plunge, he figured a few more were certain to follow and that we had just enough money to wait for them to arrive. The problem was this: just enough money is never enough money.

In fact, just enough money is the *worst* amount of money.

The obvious reason for this is that it's stressful. Research from Eldar Shafir, a Princeton psychologist, found that scarcity-related stress doesn't simply change the way you feel, but it changes the way you think. In his studies on low-income populations, he finds that what can appear like short-sighted or irresponsible financial decisions are often the result of "bandwidth poverty"—the inability to plan long term, driven by the constant need to solve immediate problems. He states,

> *When so many moments of the day require your full attention, there's very little of it left to worry about things that are not right in front of your eyes . . . and then you start doing things you wish you hadn't done. You don't quite remember to do things in time. You don't anticipate things that are going to happen tomorrow.* [42]

While your mom may give you some money because she loves you, your venture investor won't. They invest because you convince them you can build the future. But building the future is hard to do if you can't see past today.

Of all the things I wish I could do over, properly capitalizing the business is at the top of my list. The cost of significant dilution early would have been nothing compared to the significant cost of myopia

---

42   Excerpt from an NPR interview with Eldar Shafir performed by Laura Starecheski on *All Things Considered.*

that later ensued. At Dealstruck, I was always solving a crisis, always running out of cash, always saving the company. I've heard this called Hero Leadership, but it's no form of leadership at all. Under these conditions, what look like solutions are simply Band-Aids. For a while, I was naive enough to pride myself on having done more, faster, cheaper—what the Valley refers to as "hacking." Yet, every time I applied a short-term fix to a long-term problem, I unwittingly incurred a debt (pun intended) that I'd one day be unable to repay.

The biggest problem of being bandwidth poor is that you don't know you're impoverished—you're not aware you're making short-sighted decisions, you're making the only decisions you can see. It's only in hindsight—when the future you couldn't envision becomes the present you face—that you realize the supposedly sensible decisions you made along the way were anything but. We've all experienced this before—this "How did I get here?" moment. Maybe it's a drug addiction, maybe a criminal offense or an unhealthy relationship. Or, if you're like me, maybe it's your startup.

All this is to say that being poor is actually quite expensive. If you can pay up now to avoid it later, you should.

Given that I'd been feeling the "cognitive tax" of chronic under-capitalization for the better part of four years, the fact we'd come into money didn't entice me to waste energy on anything other than landing TAB. Which leads me to the second, less obvious, problem of having just enough dough: your venture investors will want to spend it.

Rolling the dice is logical for them. Dealstruck was one of dozens, if not hundreds, of investments within Trinity's portfolio. Losing their $9m was disappointing—perhaps angering—but, it was the venture business model operating in ordinary course. Though venture portfolios tend to be diversified (i.e. they consist of many "little" bets), their returns are remarkably concentrated (i.e. few pay off, but they pay off big). Aware of their economic reality, VCs consistently operate with the objective of finding a "fund maker"—an investment yielding a return significant enough to render obsolete the outcomes of all others in the fund. A by-product of their search for this Holy Grail is indifference as to whether, on their losers, they lose $9m or $12m—if they do it right, it's a rounding error in the end. The irony here is that in venture investing the appropriate way to *manage* risk is almost always to take *more* of it.

As renowned venture investor Fred Wilson once said about his early track-record of success:[43]

> *I remember back in the mid 90s, I used to say with some pride that I had not lost money on any of my VC investments. Then one day, someone told me "then you are not taking enough risk." I ended that streak of not losing money on VC investments in the late 90s in a series of epic flameouts . . . But I learned a lot from them. Not only was my "winning streak" a case of not taking enough risk, it was also a case of not enough learning.*

The same concept exists in lending—if you aren't losing money, you are leaving too much of it on the table. But there are two ways to lose money—by frequency and by severity. The former refers to how *often* a loss occurs. The latter refers to how *big* the loss is when it does. The product of these equals total loss. For example, if 10 percent of your loans default (frequency) and the loss-given-default is 50 percent (severity), your total losses will be 5 percent. In lending, most really bad things are the result of severity (see Ch. 11) and investing more to avoid loss almost always results in more of it (see Ch. 15). Prudent lenders (the hypocrisy is not lost on me) obsess about not having a big loss, while prudent venture capitalists obsess about the opposite—not having a big gain. One big loss can kill a lender, even if the rest of the portfolio performs perfectly, whereas one big gain can make a VC, even if the rest of the portfolio performs poorly.

Despite Noel's inherent bias toward swinging for the fences, he was adamant he wouldn't "throw caution to the wind if there were

---

43   Brad Feld, "Do You Regret Failed Investments?" *FeldThoughts,* April 8, 2016, http://www.feld.com/archives/2016/04/regret-failed-investments.html

no other options."

I had been clear that it was TAB or bust, but Noel never recovered trust in me after my "ill-timed" Spain trip a year earlier. Though our mess bore Z's fingerprints too, Noel perceived him as the lesser of two evils and made it habit to validate with him anything I said before accepting it as true. So, when I brought the term sheet to the Board and told them it was the best we could do, Noel turned to Z and said, "Is that true?"

Zalman knew it was.

He had told me as much many times over during our months on life support. But when he came face-to-face with a deal that would convert his unrealized loss into a realized one, he changed his tune.

I sensed this was coming. Just before TAB issued a term sheet, Z and I had flown to Ogden, Utah to instill in them some urgency (a word foreign to most bankers). There, TAB previewed the economics on offer. In all likelihood, Z would get nothing. Though he had written off his equity long ago, he held out hope that his Sub Debt would be repaid. For this to happen, every other note-holder would need to be paid back in full first—a recovery in excess of 80 percent. When TAB revealed its terms—an upfront repayment to our senior lender and an earn-out that, under the best of circumstances, would recover the Sub Debt 75 percent—Z was visibly shaken.

Z wasn't one to express emotion; in over three years working together, I'd seen him do so only twice (CAN Capital, Series A). The cab ride back to the airport in Salt Lake City was the third.

"I know you think this is a bad outcome for you, but it's worse for me," he said, staring at the seatback in front of him. "I'm fucked."

The combination of a venture capitalist indifferent to losing it all and a Board chairman who already had didn't improve our odds of winning the lottery, but it did make buying a ticket inevitable.

If you ask Z to name the person he most admires, he'll tell you it's Albert Einstein. Z had a childish fondness for Einstein he expressed regularly by wearing aged t-shirts bearing pictures, quotes, and concepts of the famed scientist. I don't know much about Einstein's definition of quantum mechanics or relativity theory, but I do know his definition of insanity: "doing the same thing over and over again and expecting different results."

Though Z harbored no doubts that I'd canvassed the capital markets completely in search of a superior outcome, when Noel asked him to affirm as much, he wavered—"Maybe we can do better." Noel then asked Z to take a second whack, incentivizing him with a promise to invest $2m into whatever deal he could gin up that wasn't TAB. Whether Z was saving face or truly impaired, I'm not sure—we were both operating under massive mental strain—but, he took the challenge, heading off to make the same ask, to the same investors, with the same set of facts (to which he, unsurprisingly, would receive the same answers).

I was furious. How could two guys—both of whom were competent, experienced, and informed—turn their backs on what was so blatantly the right thing?

Here's how: the Board's job is not to do the right thing. At least not in the moralistic sense.

Board directors have two main duties—a duty of care and a duty of loyalty. To exercise care is for them to make reasonably informed, rational judgments in good faith without the presence of a conflict of interest. To exercise loyalty is for them to act "in the best interests of the corporation and its shareholders, and to refrain from engaging in activities that permit them to receive an improper personal benefit from their relationship with the corporation."[44]

When a company is solvent—meaning it's worth more than the amount it owes to creditors—it's obvious these duties run to the shareholders, but as a company inches toward insolvency, things get pretty fuzzy. So fuzzy, in fact, that corporate attorneys (who managed to fill thirty-one pages of our first credit agreement with definitions) are yet unable to define the so-called "zone of insolvency." In theory,

---

44   Marshall Huebner and Hugh McCullough, "The Fiduciary Duties of Directors of Troubled U.S. Companies: Emerging Clarity," *ICLG To: Corporate Recovery and Insolvency*, ch. 2 (2008): 6–12.

entering this zone marks the point at which the fiduciary duties of directors progressively shift from shareholders to creditors. But in practice, plotting one's location within this vortex is so complex and imprecise that courts have dispensed with the concept altogether. Even when it's clear you're reaching the insolvent end of this zone— what's been termed "deepening insolvency"—it's a toss-up, as one court opined, "because catchy though the term may be, it does not express a coherent concept."[45]

The ultimate meaning of all this gobbledygook is that when you see a clear path to save your creditors, save your employees, save your vision, and save your reputation, the propriety of that path will be anything but clear in the eyes of the law.

More than once I'd advocate for TAB as being good for our lenders, and more than once I'd be reminded sternly that duties of officers and directors are to the shareholders.

This was insane.

The only reason we still had Board duties was because our senior lender (DLI) tripled-down and because our Sub Debt effectively converted to equity, both doing so on the promise that if we could land TAB, we would. If this wasn't the epitome of insolvent, I don't know what was. Our attorneys kept telling me that we owed our creditors "good faith," but no legal duty, which basically meant that after being honest, transparent, and forthright, we could steamroll them if they let us. After all, these were big boys (and girls), and if they didn't want to give us more leash they could say no. Thus far, they hadn't, but not on the basis of cold calculation, rather, on the basis of my word. I had more than thirty uncoordinated lenders facing a situation of immense complexity with incomplete information and they'd let us run on my assurance that when the time came to do the right thing, I would.

The time had come. I tried to do the right thing. But I couldn't act alone. So, rather than sign the term sheet while we had enough cash left to close, the Board decided to wait.

---

45   *Trenwick America Litigation Trust v. Ernst & Young, L.L.P., et. al.,* Case No. 1571-N (Del. Ch. Aug. 10, 2006).

That "time kills all deals" was not a foreign concept to a team in the deal-making business, so it didn't go unnoticed that eight months had passed since we kicked off our raise with nothing to show for it. Even if our team had remained aloof for some time, by August 3rd, 2016—the date we received TAB's initial offer in writing—that would have changed.

One month prior, as people returned from their July 4th holiday, we did a second round of layoffs. By this time the entire industry had very publicly downsized, which made our victims more understanding, but our survivors no less concerned. Unlike the prior cut, this one came with a heavy dose of reality. I told our team, "We have six months to reach cash-flow positive. We may end up with more time, but we can't count on it. We have to control our own destiny."

It's always a crapshoot whether news like this will be received as a rallying cry or a white flag. In an effort to induce commitment rather than resignation, I carefully selected language that tended toward optimism; I spoke slowly and clearly to project unwavering confidence; and I outlined specific, achievable actions that would bring us nearer to our goal (I say "nearer" because getting to cash-flow positive was a pipe-dream without concessions from DLI they'd already definitively stated they wouldn't give). Though the room was muted, I saw heads nodding, which I assumed to mean my masterfully manicured message had gotten through clearly. But what *you say* and what *they hear* are probably more different than you think. In less than twenty-four hours I learned as much when my managers relayed to me that I had their teams at "We have . . .", but I'd lost them by ". . . six months." First impressions usually take seven seconds; I hadn't gotten to seven words.

We needed to regain focus in the worst way and there was no better mechanism to accomplish this than to manufacture a quick win. In many cases, identifying quick wins is like searching for change between the couch cushions—hard to find and unlikely to be worth much. But, sometimes you get lucky and find a fifty-dollar bill laying on the sidewalk right as you walk by.

Like its techie-disruptor counterparts, Dealstruck had taken to the time-honored Silicon Valley tradition of trying to win on user experience by replacing the "nickel-and-dime" pricing model with the "no hidden fee" model. In doing this, however, we also had taken to the time-honored Silicon Valley tradition of not making money. Fintech lenders had made a bad habit of covering out-of-pocket costs, waiving fees, and reducing prices to uphold the perception that borrowers *loved* owing money to us, but *hated* owing money to our predecessors.

I remember one high-profile competitor touting a Net Promoter Score (NPS)—the preferred bellwether of customer satisfaction in the Valley—in excess of 70. NPS is calculated by asking customers, "On a scale from 1–10, how likely are you to recommend this product or service to others?" Add up your nines and tens ("promoters"), subtract your zeroes through sixes ("detractors"), then divide this difference by the total number people surveyed. Basic algebra will demonstrate a score of 70 to mean my competitor claimed nearly all of its customers would recommend borrowing online from them at 50 percent APR, when less than half as many would recommend doing so for a lot less from their local bank (average NPS for the banking industry was 32).[46]

I'm sure NPS sticklers will tell me I'm oversimplifying and mis-interpreting—they are a puritanical bunch—but, I'm also sure an overwhelming majority of people wouldn't recommend borrowing money, no matter who it's from.

There's an old joke among economists: if there was really a $20 bill in the street someone would have picked it up already; the corollary is there is no "free lunch." Given our circumstances, however, continuing to walk past free lunch money today wasn't an option even if, in the long-run, it wasn't exactly free; so we bent down to pick it up. Rolling out a "traditional" set of fees wasn't a win in itself, but the $100k of incremental income it produced thirty days later was.

---

46   Temkin Group, "Net Promoter Score Benchmark Study, 2016," October 2016, http://temkingroup.com/research-reports/net-promoter-score-benchmark-study-2016/

For a moment, we celebrated. But things were far from good.

Zalman was coming up empty on his last-ditch wild-goose chase and the Board still hadn't moved forward on the TAB term sheet.

It was now early October. In the more than sixty days since we'd received TAB's offer, only two things of import had happened:

1) We burned half our runway

2) The deal got worse

Technically, the deal didn't get worse for us—it got worse for our lender, DLI. In its initial construct, TAB intended to purchase our loan portfolio by paying DLI the full amount it was owed by Dealstruck. But after a few more months of bad numbers fucked up what little good story we had left (see Ch. 8), this price dropped a few percentage points. On the money DLI was owed, they would now be in-the-hole a couple million dollars at closing, recouping this amount over time via their pole position on the earn-out.[47]

My math hadn't changed—this deal still needed to happen—but DLI's math had. Though they could expect to recover everything owed to them within two years (the earn-out would more than cover the shortfall), any amounts not paid upfront would have to be recorded on their books as a write-off. And, DLI didn't like to do write-offs.

I was stuck.

If DLI wouldn't accept a discount, TAB wouldn't proceed. Despite issuing multiple warnings to Brendan that, under any circumstance, he'd be in for more pain without TAB than with them, he wasn't budging.

So, I signaled to the bullpen and out came none other than the TAB CEO himself. Earlier in the negotiating process, Curt had indicated, in what would prove to be a remarkable display of false bravado, that if we couldn't twist Brendan's arm, he'd be happy to. In need of some outside muscle, I arranged an arm-wrestling match

---

47   Despite being our senior lender, DLI was actually second in line. In the process of playing Musical Lenders, we had to win a concession from Vincent, our highest net-worth investor, that required jumping him to the front of the line (with DLI's consent) on a small portion of his investment.

at Brendan's Los Angeles-based office on a Friday in early October.

The day before our tri-party meeting, I called Curt to arm him with as much ammunition as I could to help him force Brendan into submission. Perhaps this was an act of treason—recall, the fiduciary issues were complex—but, I didn't care. When my sister was little, my mom tricked her into taking her medicine by crushing bitter pills into Cool Whip and strawberries, disguising it as a tasty dessert. Honest, no. But all for the better, yes. Machiavellian tactics don't make for great long-term business relationships, but when you're making your final stand, defecting is always the dominant strategy.

Though I had handed Curt the answer key before the final exam, he still managed to fail. By no means am I a world-class negotiator, but his was the most stunning display of negotiating incompetence I'd ever witnessed. An abbreviated version follows:

CURT: *We like this company.*
BRENDAN: *If you want the company, pay me off.*
CURT: *No.*
BRENDAN: *But it's a really good company.*
CURT: *Fine, we'll pay you off.*

It took a few hours for this interchange to unfold, but by the end of it, DLI was getting paid in full, the earn-out economics were improved, and, everyone, including Curt, was smiling and laughing.

Everyone except me, that is.

In basketball, there is a phenomenon known as a "toilet bowl" shot. This refers to a ball that circles the rim multiple times before finally resolving to drop in the basket for two points or to bounce out for zero. Our salespeople sometimes encountered similar situations—what I'll call a "toilet bowl" deal. These deals were orbiting the rim—practically in the basket—but, absent one final nudge, could still spin off in the wrong direction. To help our salespeople slam these deals shut, we allowed them (coincidentally) two percentage points of pricing leeway without requiring resubmission to

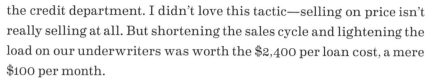

the credit department. I didn't love this tactic—selling on price isn't really selling at all. But shortening the sales cycle and lightening the load on our underwriters was worth the $2,400 per loan cost, a mere $100 per month.

Delegating pricing authority over two-and-a-half-*thousand* dollars is one thing, but delegating it over two-and-a-half-*million* is another. Sure, TAB was bigger than us, but not *that* much bigger. So, when Curt conceded on price to seal the deal, my experience informed me he had used more than his allotted two points.

At Dealstruck, sales could push a loan to the finish line, but if they stepped out of bounds, it wouldn't make it across. This was the fate I feared: that when it came time to close, TAB's Board never would.

As our meeting wound to completion, I, in disbelief, considered restating the accord to ensure everyone was on the same page before parting ways. But I didn't. At that moment, TAB was happy, DLI was happy, and, most importantly, Zalman was happy, too. Under the revised terms, his Sub Debt had a chance. Never mind the inevitable renegotiation that awaited down the road, I had to get my Board in the car and buckled up before that would matter. If I had Z, I had Noel. So long as I bit my tongue, right now I had them both.

On the drive home, Z and I couldn't get more than a few miles from DLI's office before Brendan called in a bewildered frenzy, "Can you believe that guy? I didn't even have to negotiate; all I had to do is let him keep talking."

After three months of anger, hostility, and disagreement, Z and I were reunited. Though we buried the hatchet on the car ride home, I had, through this process, seen parts of Z I couldn't unsee; I'm guessing he'd say the same. Our relationship would recover, but it would never be the same. Stuck in LA traffic on our way south to San Diego, he glanced at me through one side of his sunglasses and asked, "Do you feel a bit better now?"

"Yes, but only a bit," I said.

We'd sign the TAB term sheet the following week, but Noel's distrust and Zalman's disillusion had cost us dearly. In forty-five days, we'd be broke, and not a single lawyer had yet put pen to paper. I'd finally gotten a yes, but it was too slow. All I could hope was that it wasn't too late.

adios,
mi amor

IT'S BEEN SAID that behind every great man there is a great woman. But even the not-so-great man is sometimes struck by dumb luck—I certainly was. That my personal life was ascendant while my professional life crumbled was the only thing keeping me from sliding into debilitating depression and keeping my company from capitulating under mounting stress.

To the unskilled logician, these simultaneous, yet opposing arcs of love and loss might imply a causal link—I know Maria felt this way at times ("it's all my fault, isn't it?"). However, nothing could be further from the truth. Without Maria I would have been broken. Nothing did more to raise my spirits, strengthen my resolve, and restore my will every day than waking up next to her and hearing her whisper three words before I plunged into battle: "Adios, mi amor."

Among the psychological shortcomings that afflict entrepreneurs—and there are many[48]—narcissism might be the most prominent. While these bugs may be considered features in your

---

48 Arrogance, psychopathy, and narcissism, and their connection to entrepreneurship, are discussed by German researchers in a 2011 article on Gigaom and by Claudia Kalb, a medical and science journalist, in a 2016 interview with the *Harvard Business Review*.

quest for success, they're likely taking a silent toll on the people you love the most, and who you will be too self-consumed to notice or to care about. The most amazing thing is that, despite your self-absorption, these people will shower you with sympathy, wrap you with warmth, and bend over backwards to ease your pain even while you remain wholly ignorant of theirs. This adulation should appease the narcissists' need for attention and affirmation, but it probably won't. In fact, it might make things worse.

Why?

Because a core tenet of the entrepreneurial ethos is that you can't understand the entrepreneur's plight unless you've been one. As your friends wish you success, as your family praises your efforts, as your lover lauds your courage, you'll probably be insulted— maybe even a bit angry—that *normal* people would dare presume they can understand what you're going through. Unfortunately, this arrogance is as common as it is hypocritical. This is narcissism at its finest: a "grandiose sense of importance, preoccupation with unlimited success, [and a] belief that one is special . . . "[49]

Here's a truth that will seem anything but true while you're trying to change the world: your business isn't special, but their unconditional love is.

I'm not suggesting entrepreneurship isn't a noble endeavor, nor am I suggesting it's wrong to care deeply about what you do. I'm merely suggesting you are not the only one paying a price for it, and if you're too ignorant of this for too long, you could end up losing the only things in life you can't slap a valuation on. This may not matter to you. That's okay. To some of the world's "greatest" entrepreneurs, it didn't. To me, it did.

So, when it came time to head back to Spain—even as we were running out of money, even as we were squabbling over the term sheet, and even after doing so one year prior had cost me my credibility— I went.

---

49   Steve Bressert, "Narcissistic Personality Disorder Symptoms," *PsychCentral,* September 8, 2017, https://psychcentral.com/disorders/narcissistic-personality-disorder-symptoms/

Two days after arriving in Spain, we finalized the term sheet and Z signed it on my behalf. Two days after that, TAB Bank would be on site. This left me twenty-four hours to figure out how to tell my team.

Communicating an acquisition widely so early in the closing process isn't common practice. Typically, you try to limit the number of people "under the tent" while you iron out all the gory details with your future bosses. There are at least two good reasons for doing this: first, to avoid distracting line-level employees who keep the gears of your business in motion; and second, to avoid looking like a clown if the deal falls apart, which could leave you stuck at a town-hall in front of one-hundred twenty nervous eyeballs delivering the punchline in the world's worst joke—"just kidding!"

Sadly, we didn't have this luxury.

Despite TAB's multiple attempts to access my team before issuing a term sheet, I had rebuffed their every effort,[50] leery of fueling unnecessary company-wide speculation before extracting a commitment. Now that they'd proposed, there was no way to consummate our marriage without affording them an opportunity to meet the family first. Add to this the fact we were running on fumes, and we had no choice but to accede to their every request at once. If we were going to close this deal—and it was a big *if*—we needed diligence and documentation to converge miraculously before our quite-literal deadline. Rather than let my team draw their own conclusions about what a bunch of TAB guys running around our office implied for their future, I decided to beat them to it. If you lose control of the narrative, I've found it's quite hard to get it back.

I think The Exit is every entrepreneur's dream, but when it comes, it may not be how you dreamed it. I'd envisioned triumph— champagne, high-fives, employees arguing over which luxury car to buy, and maybe a few tears of joy from executives whose lives were changed forever. But my Exit would be nothing like that. TAB was a

---

50 Some of my management team met with TAB the day they first came to visit, but I insisted we were discussing a marketing partnership. It's a thinly veiled excuse, but the best I had.

lifeline and lifelines are never gold-plated. No one would be getting anything except a job, if they were "lucky"—which is exactly what concerned me as I prepared to break the news.

Most people had joined Dealstruck because it wasn't *just* a job. Whether my supposedly lucky colleagues would see themselves as such when their grand prize was an offer of employment from a no-name bank whose main selling point was a 401(k) match and a Ping-Pong table wasn't clear to me. If my team, or key members of it, walked, TAB would walk too. As uninspired as I was by the transaction, whatever I said had to be inspiring.

Via Skype, from the south of Spain, I delivered a ten-minute monologue stressing the value TAB placed on our *people* (read: you have a job), our *independence* (read: it's still not *just* a job), and our *growth* (read: this job still could be lucrative). I told them that I was excited and couldn't imagine a better partner; that we were the forerunners of a new industry paradigm in which bank and non-bank converge into one; that this was a big win.

If people saw through my forced smile or my feigned enthusiasm, they didn't act like it. Perhaps I'd become too jaded by Wall Street opportunism or Silicon Valley talent wars—where a slightly bigger paycheck, a slightly better benefits package, and a slightly larger stock grant was enough to convince the most loyal employee to abandon ship for the competition—to remember that people are motivated by things other than money. Dan Ariely, a famed behavioral economist, has studied workplace motivation in depth and concluded:

> *When we think about labor, we usually think about motivation and payment as the same thing, but the reality is that we should probably add all kinds of things to it: meaning, creation, challenges, ownership, identity, pride, etc.*[51]

The harder the challenge, the more pride we develop. The deeper the purpose, the more committed we are. The greater the

---

51   Dan Ariely. TED Talk: What makes us feel good about our work?

acknowledgment, the more rewarded we feel. That I'd feared a mutiny when my team found out our stock options were worthless turned out to be a projection of my own resignation. My team still felt proud, my team still felt committed, and, with TAB, my team felt, in some fashion, rewarded. I didn't. After more than four years of pouring everything into my company, Dealstruck was just a job. And, a pretty shitty one at that.

After the announcement, I placed a few one-on-one phone calls to team members who I thought might need more reassurance. But again, I was projecting. Everyone was thrilled that we'd made it somewhere, *anywhere*. I guess when you've been floating in the middle of the ocean, the sight of dry land—inhabitable or not—is enough. My colleagues offered me congratulations. They asked me how I felt—if I was happy. I responded candidly, "Happy, no. Relieved, yes."

As I sat on the patio absorbing the day's events under a clear night-sky, I lost myself in a reflective moment I'd denied myself for years on end (as with most hair-raising endeavors, it's best not to think about them too much while you're in the act). In looking back, I could recall times at Dealstruck where I felt exhilarated, brave, and even accomplished, but I struggled to recall times where I felt truly happy. The old saying about boat ownership came to mind—I was happy the day my business started, and I'd be happy the day it ended.

Happiness isn't the only emotion worth feeling—the diversity of our senses is what makes life livable—but if it's the biggest part of what you are looking for, you might not find it in your startup.

Though I'd begun to reminisce, I was doing so prematurely. We had a term sheet and a motivated buyer, but a deal's never done until it's done.

One day after I informed my team of our impending sale, TAB arrived on site with a six-person due diligence crew led by its CEO, Curt. Standing in front of sixty eager onlookers, Curt opened the ceremonies with an impassioned monologue about Dealstruck's central role in transforming TAB into a technology-first bank-of-the-future for small businesses. Curt wasn't a great public speaker—years of smoking had supplanted his "um" with a labored cough—but his presence alone did all it needed to do: convince people this was real. After his speech concluded, each of my team members, at Zalman's suggestion, walked up to Curt, introduced themselves, and shook his hand. They may have thought they were merely brown-nosing the new kingpin, but buyers need comfort too. Z's clever orchestration told TAB, "we are *all* all-in."

Despite our being all-in, the ten days of silence that followed TAB's hasty victory lap had me fearful they were not. Before they could back out, I had to take care of one urgent matter.

From the first day I met Maria, her biggest concern was that I'd be successful and become a startup douche-bag with more money and ego than humility and kindness. My entire life, I'd operated under a modified version of Descartes's famed philosophical supposition—*I achieve, therefore I am.* That there was something of value underlying my being, absent achievement, was a foreign concept to me. The existential question that I feared most was, *If I don't achieve, what will I be?* Maria feared the opposite, *If he does achieve, what will he become?*

In my high-school days, I had a female friend who was too much of a spiritual-hippy-flower girl to arouse in me anything more than platonic interest, but who introduced me to a poem titled *Desiderata,* by Max Ehrmann. The poem reads a bit like a secular prayer and, like most prayers, saying the words is easy, but believing them isn't. After I'd spent thirty years searching for external validation, loving Maria made these words ring true:

> *You are a child of the universe,*
> *no less than the trees and the stars;*
> *you have a right to be here.*

There is no way to repay someone who awakens within you a sense of permanence and belonging on no basis other than blood flowing through your veins and air flowing through your lungs, but asking her to marry you is a start. I wasn't planning to propose before the TAB deal. But when I caught myself in a fallacy—if we closed the deal, I *deserved* her hand in marriage; if we closed the company, I didn't—I knew it was time. If it was true that I had a right to be here, it was equally true I wanted her with me as long as I was.

I don't share this story to brag about my wife or to bring some romance into an otherwise clinical tale. Rather, I share it to highlight critical psychological flaws in my first attempt at entrepreneurship—inadequate perspective, improper motivation, interminable worry—that carried significant emotional tolls, if not financial ones. I can assure you whatever great fear you harbor won't manifest itself in failure, just as whatever great hope you await won't reveal itself in success. Energy spent worrying about either is energy you don't have to waste. For better, for worse, for richer, for poorer, in sickness and health, in good times and bad, you are not your startup.

Despite my brief jaunt into the mystical, you don't need to believe in divine equilibrium to understand that really great news is usually followed by less great news (and vice-versa). Statisticians call this phenomenon "regression to the mean," and it's primarily responsible for why things are never quite as good or quite as bad as they seem. It's also the reason entrepreneurship has an addictive quality that leaves even the most insistent "I can quit any time I want" users more unable to do so than they think—just when we're about to kick our habit, we get our next high. If proposing to Maria was my highest of highs, it was only fitting that what followed was my lowest of lows.

TAB was out.

During the fateful early October meeting in which TAB acquiesced to DLI's every demand, Curt left thinking he was still getting a bargain, but his Board didn't share the sentiment. In our haste to sign the term sheet, we left in brackets (an indication of a deal point not yet finalized) the one item we thought we had settled—the structure and purchase price of the loan portfolio from DLI. Though we had come to a handshake agreement a few weeks prior, such an agreement isn't much use if you're not shaking the right hand. Whether Curt was overaggressive by design didn't matter—he had no reason to be the bad cop when his Board would do the dirty work for him.

There is a maxim in athletic training that you must "go slow to go fast." The basic concept is that bursts of peak performance or maximum power are only attainable if you recover properly in between them. There is no more certain way to dull the top-end of your output than to run as fast as you can all the time. For the high achiever—athlete or entrepreneur—this cadence is extremely counter-intuitive. We always want to be on the gas; we fear easing up may relegate us to first-gear forever. Our burden is to exert as much energy into recovery—into slowing down—as most people exert in doing the opposite. It won't be pleasant, but it will be worth it.

Term sheets are a prime example of when going fast will slow you down. We see the deal. We want to close. Our instincts tell us, "Let's sign this thing and get on with it; we can pin the details down later." Remember, *go slow to go fast*. Blowing through brackets or blank spaces can lead to congestion in closing—if not a crash—but, a tap on the brakes will get you home safely. Though I'd hit bumper-to-bumper traffic before—with Brevet and with Echelon—I had yet to be in a collision. (Eight years ago I was riding shotgun in my friend's brand-new Mini Cooper as he dodged in-and-out of heavy SoCal freeway traffic. I said I felt unsafe and he responded, "Don't worry, I've never had an accident." Months later, he had a new car, having wrecked the other one.)

The benefits (speed, safety, cost) that arise from modifying a seven-page term sheet instead of a seventy-page financing document are particularly important if you're running an early-stage company, since your urgency will exponentially outgrow your investor's or acquirer's as time passes. This isn't *always* the case—perhaps you'll find yourself with time and options, or find a desperate Partner in "deal heat." More likely, though, you'll find yourself with every reason *to* close while your counterpart has every reason *not* to. In a business where the best deals are often the ones never done, playing chicken with your investor isn't a wise bet.

In the case of TAB, we had no choice but to sign an incomplete document. For one, we were (literally) out of time. But more importantly, the incomplete item wasn't ours to negotiate. The portfolio purchase price was for TAB and DLI to resolve and their manner of doing so was to engage in a high-stakes chicken-fight over the following question—who would hurt more if Dealstruck went under?

The calculus was obvious.

Without a deal, TAB would continue as a small, family-owned bank with a profitable niche and an assured future. DLI, on the other hand, might not have a future. Aside from the "expected losses" (i.e. known and reasonably estimable) already in its portfolio, DLI relied on our team for loan servicing, a critical function for minimizing future loss. If we became unable to service loans or if our clients became aware of our winding down, DLI's losses might spike, potentially challenging the fund's long-term viability.

On multiple phone calls over the past few months, I tried persuading Brendan to take an inch or two off the top today—by accepting a discounted payoff—to avoid a buzz cut later. But he was unfazed. "If the TAB deal falls through," he said, "I'm making enough money on my other investments to fund Dealstruck myself." I warned him things would be worse than he expected; I warned him neither Z nor I would run a zombie company; I warned him there was no other end in sight. Regardless of what I threw at him, it was never enough. I simply couldn't make him understand that the consequences of our failure would likely expose his fund to more risk than whatever alternatives he was imagining.

So, Brendan held his ground. Until, on a Friday evening in mid-November, 2016, when he finally panicked. I called to share with him the ultimatum I had issued to TAB earlier in the day: commit to a closing timeline[52] by Monday at 12:00 p.m. PT or I'd lay everyone off the following morning. The gig was up.

Brendan was silent. Then he said, "You can't do this to me. I am, like, literally staring over the edge. My life is over."

"I have an idea," I told him.

---

52   We targeted a year-end close, but to do so we needed TAB to commit to the transaction so documentation could begin. I was not asking them to close the transaction by Monday; I was asking them, by Monday, to affirm with confidence they would close on the agreed-upon timetable.

If Dealstruck shut down, DLI would be forced to incur expenses associated with an orderly transition of its loan portfolio to a new servicer. I suggested to Brendan he'd be better off incurring those costs to *avoid* a transition than to facilitate one. He agreed.

That Sunday at 9:00 p.m. PT, I called Curt with Brendan on the line. It was Hail Mary time. "Curt," I said, "I've spoken to Brendan. He can't offer you a discount on his loans, but he can offer you $1.5m over twelve months to offset your integration costs."

That's right, TAB—the buyer—was *getting paid* to close the deal.

It was too late. TAB's Board had moved on. The following day at lunchtime I received formal notice from Curt—TAB was withdrawing from the term sheet.

There is a famous psychology experiment in which participants are handed lottery tickets numbering 361204, 965304, or 865305. After the winning number is revealed to be 865304, the participants are surveyed as to their level of frustration. Without fail, the first ticket-holders rank the least upset and the last ticket-holders rank the most.[53] Despite each ticket having an identical probability of being a winner—and, conversely, of being a loser—the unlucky recipients of a ticket more closely resembling the winner experience the pain of defeat disproportionately.

Mathematically, a near-miss shouldn't hurt more than missing-by-a-mile, but it does.

The experiment above is one illustration of the Simulation Heuristic, a term coined by behavioral scientists Daniel Kahneman and Amos Tversky.[54] The first part posits that people determine the likelihood of an event based on the ease with which the event can be imagined. In other words, the closer reality is (865304) to some desirable alternative (865305), the more probable we deem the alternative

53   Daniel Kahneman and Amos Tversky, "The Psychology of Preferences," *Scientific American* (January 1982): 136–142.

54   Though the research on the Simulation Heuristic was published by Kahneman and Tversky in 1981, I drew some of my discussion from Michael Lewis's 2016 book, *The Undoing Project: A Friendship That Changed Our Minds,* that details the history of the relationship between the famed research partners.

to have been even if, mathematically, it was equally as likely as any other (361204). The second part of the heuristic posits that our resulting frustration with reality will be the product of "the possibility of the alternative" and "the desirability of the alternative." This means missing the lottery by one digit hurts more than missing it by three, but also that missing a $200m lottery by one digit hurts more than missing a $200 lottery by the same amount.

Put simply, when the alternative appears both close and highly desirable, we're in for a world of pain.

There were a thousand ways we could have died over the prior eighteen months, but the fact we were one signature away from rescue really stung. We'd raised a bridge when no one thought we could; our team stayed together when no one thought it would; our lender kept us afloat when no one thought it should. And, although our financial winnings would have been a pittance, selling the business looked like a damn big jackpot when the next-best option was a burial.

As I hung up the phone with Curt, a wave of shame, embarrassment, anger, and sadness washed over me. But there would be time for mourning later. We had a busy twenty-four hours ahead of us. The next morning, I wouldn't only be hearing "Adios, mi amor," I'd be saying it, too.

CHAPTER 18

'til death
do us part

WINDING DOWN A FINANCE COMPANY isn't like shuttering a bakery—you can't simply stop the ovens and put up a "closed" sign. The main reason for this relates to all the pastries still lying around which, in our case, consisted of nearly one thousand outstanding loans we couldn't let go stale; they needed to be repaid. While we would have liked to toss them in the garbage or donate them to a shelter, loans are living, breathing things that need other living, breathing things bugging them to make sure they abide by the terms of their contracts. So, when it came time to say goodbye, we couldn't say goodbye to everyone at once.

In the weeks leading up to our D-Day, Zalman, Robert, and I had constructed a relatively robust business continuity plan (BCP) that, unlike most such plans, didn't have anything to do with continuity at all—this was a disaster plan (hence the D in D-Day). That we called it a BCP was a belt-and-suspenders maneuver to protect ourselves from inadvertently exposing its true nature to an unwitting passerby who might glance at our screens or beat us to the printer.

We split this plan into two segments—the Leavers and the Stayers. Let's take the Stayers first.

Think about a mortgage. A homeowner owns a home, but pledges it to a lender in case of default. Should the homeowner be unable to repay, the lender can foreclose on the home and try to monetize it in a manner sufficient to cover its outstanding balance. Once the lender—usually a bank—takes the home, they may engage service providers to maintain or appraise its value, or to properly market it, but the costs of doing so and any ultimate shortfall accrue to them directly. The homeowner's credit gets whacked, but they are otherwise out of the picture. The same thing happens with a finance company, but instead of owning a home, we owned a loan portfolio.

When we could no longer pay as agreed, DLI foreclosed on its loans and sought to retain—at its own expense—a dramatically slimmed-down version of Dealstruck to service the portfolio through the transition to a more stable servicer. Hence, the Stayers.

The Stayers were under no obligation to stay. I was fairly confident that moral suasion alone would convince the people I needed to ride with me to the end, but Brendan wasn't willing to take that chance. Thus, each of the ten Stayers was offered some combination of a pay raise, a retention bonus, and a severance package sufficiently rich to override whatever disinterest, disappointment, and fatigue they might feel when the Leavers left. Though the Stayers had financial incentive to stick around, I wasn't certain they all would. My heart was warmed, however, when Steve—who had once quit before he started and once resigned before he rejoined—responded to my request that he stay by saying, "It would be kinda fucked up if I didn't." I'm sure I was searching especially hard for silver-linings, but it was at least mild consolation to see that my team cared enough about their work and each other to finish what they started.

It also helped that the Leavers weren't getting much of anything on their way out. Though we saved enough money to cover final payrolls, paid time off (PTO) accruals, and administrative wind-down costs, we could barely scrounge up two weeks of severance after playing out our cards with TAB. So, aside from one extra paycheck, the Leavers' exit packages mostly consisted of "how-to" guides relating to unemployment benefits, medical coverage, and resume preparation. Although these items can't be redeemed for cash, I don't want to minimize the importance of having this information packaged in a complete and coherent fashion.

There is a famous study in which two sets of colonoscopy patients undergo identical procedures save for the speed with which the probe is removed upon completion. One group has the probe removed quickly, but painfully. The other group has the probe removed slowly, but far less painfully. Even though the cumulative amount and duration of pain is greater for the latter group, they report experiencing far less discomfort than the former.[55] This is part of what psychologists call the Peak-end Rule that, stated briefly, finds, "An event makes its mark in our memories more by what happens at its end than at any prior point."[56]

Doing whatever you can to ease people into joblessness is not only the right thing to do, it's good business. If you can't leave people with money, you can still leave them with a positive memory.

When it came time for action, Robert and Zalman stealthily tapped the Stayers on the shoulder and asked them to meet in a conference room away from the sales floor at 11:00 a.m. sharp. The time was 10:55 a.m. The remainder of the team—the Leavers—had already started to congregate on our sales floor for the 11:00 a.m. Town Hall to which they'd been invited earlier in the week. Once I confirmed the Stayers had vacated, I emerged from my office, called the team to attention, and read to them my favorite quotation from Roosevelt's "The Man in the Arena":

55   Donald A. Redelmeier, Joel Katz, and Daniel Kahneman, "Memories of Colonoscopy: A Randomized Trial," *Pain* 104, nos. 1–2 (2003): 187–194.

56   This concise restatement comes from "Happiness: It's All About the Ending" by Susan Krauss Whitbourne, professor of psychology at UMass-Amherst, in an article on the website Psychology Today. Credit for discovering the Peak-End Rule belongs to Daniel Kahneman and his associates in their 1993 paper published in *Psychological Science,* "When more pain is preferred to less: Adding a better end."

It is not the critic who counts; not the man who points out
how the strong man stumbles, or where the doer of deeds could
have done them better. The credit belongs to the man who is
actually in the arena, whose face is marred by dust and sweat
and blood; who strives valiantly; who errs, who comes short
again and again, because there is no effort without error and
shortcoming; but who does actually strive to do the deeds; who
knows great enthusiasms, the great devotions; who spends
himself in a worthy cause; who at the best knows in the end the
triumph of high achievement, and who at the worst, if he fails,
at least fails while daring greatly, so that his place shall never
be with those cold and timid souls who neither know victory
nor defeat.

While I read, I could see the mood transforming in slow-motion
as the absence of their teammates, the quiver in my voice, and the
content of my words made my next statement self-evident:

"Today is Dealstruck's last day as a going concern. All good
things come to an end, and today our time has come."

Some people cried, some walked away before I could finish,
some stared in disbelief, and a few marveled at their own clairvoy-
ance with a slightly-too-enthusiastic "I knew it!"

More for my own sake than theirs, I added a few remarks about
feeling pride for the thousands of small businesses we helped, for
the culture we created, and for the distance we traveled from "two
guys and a whiteboard" to this moment together. I closed with a
comment they all needed to hear before our last goodbye—this was
my failing, not theirs. Like any company, we'd had our share of bad
hires, departmental cliques, and impassioned finger-pointing, but
our downfall was not a reflection of the commitment, creativity, or
competence of any of the fifty-odd people who stood before me that
day. Every one of them deserved better.

Immediately following the announcement, as final paychecks
and paperwork were being handed out, I received a few hugs and

words of gratitude, but most people wandered aimlessly back to their desks with no sense of what they should do now. Some resumed underwriting loans or calling on prospects, not quite sure whether simply stopping was an appropriate course of action. Within an hour, though, most everyone—including the Stayers—had followed the lead of a few visionary salespeople who wasted no time locking down a local bar for a wistful afternoon of alcohol-induced storytelling.

But for a few friendly faces, the place was empty.

Painful as it was to confront my team, I was ready to rip the Band-Aid off. That afternoon, I communicated the news to all of my investors and spent the better part of the next forty-eight hours doubling as a punching bag. By this point, I had reached a level of numbness that made me impervious to body blows and knockout punches alike.

I cared deeply about my investors, but depersonalizing their sometimes personal attacks was a critical act of psychological self-preservation.

As an eight-year-old kid subconsciously blaming himself for his parents' divorce, I would often tell my dad I wanted to crawl into a hole and never come out. My despair grew to a point where he actually printed me a poster of a giant red circle with a diagonal line across it and the words, "No Holes." Unfortunately, my immaturity led me down a hole so deep I spent the better part of five years in tears, fears, and loneliness battling my way out. Twenty years later, the temptation to wallow, to self-flagellate, to atone endlessly for my failure was as strong as ever, but I fought it off by instead erecting a barrier in the form of an explanation and an apology looped mindlessly on repeat. Despite the pain of the moment, life would go on—for my investors and for me—and it's a lot easier to find your way out from behind a wall than to climb your way out from the bottom of a ditch.

If your investors throw you a shovel, I recommend not digging.

Within a couple days, the investor calls subsided, allowing me to turn my attention back to the far more familiar task of settling bills.

Even when we were operational, I'd become relatively skilled at paying late, paying less, and, in some cases, not paying at all. There is a classic *Seinfeld* episode [57] in which Kramer, offering to get George a discount on a new pair of glasses, boasts, "Retail is for suckers." George, ever the penny-pincher and in disbelief of his good fortune, asks:

GEORGE: *Wow. What do I have to do?*
KRAMER: *You just gotta mention my name.*
GEORGE: *That's it?*
KRAMER: *That's it.*

Getting a discount really is that easy, but most people are too afraid to ask for one. I can assure you, though, whatever reservations you may have about *asking* your vendors for a discount will disappear when instead you are *telling* them they're giving you one.

We had more than fifty vendors and approximately twenty-five cents on the dollar to go around. With most firms, I offered a quarter, they asked for half, I told them no, they agreed.

Negotiating is easy when there is no room to negotiate.

But there were a few firms—mostly the larger ones—who rejected my best efforts to throw money at them. With this group, a low-level receivables clerk with limited authority to settle would try to win me over by combining a 15 percent courtesy discount with the threat of further escalation, to which I responded by practically begging them to escalate me faster. I'm probably one of the few people these folks ever dealt with who awaited a collections call as eagerly as most kids await Santa Claus on Christmas Eve. I wasn't looking for a fight, I was looking for someone who would send me wire instructions so I could send them money before there was no money left to send. Ironically, big companies with bloated collections processes are the worst type of collector to deal with the best type of deadbeat. I was both willing and able to pay some amount, but I

---

57   Larry David, Jerry Seinfeld, Tom Gammill, and Max Pross, writers, "The Glasses." In *Seinfeld,* directed by Tom Cherones. NBC. September 30, 1993.

imagine most of these firms are probably still running an internal review on a settlement offer that no longer exists.

Another oddity of settling bills with large firms is that while one department will be trying to chase down payment on stuff they already sold you, another department will be trying to sell you more.

At Dealstruck, we sometimes found ourselves making the same mistake. I remember our collections team reaming out our re-marketing group (the team responsible for selling to existing customers) for accidentally calling delinquent accounts to offer additional financing, convinced this was a sign of organizational ineptitude, individual incompetence, or both. Startup employees have a way of being especially indignant at small procedural breakdowns, thinking that such elementary mix-ups would never happen at more mature institutions. The good news is your team's indignation results from their awareness of the breakdown and their ability to fix it; the bad news is, big or small, there will always be breakdowns.

Once I'd settled most of our bills, or at least tried to, the remainder of my tenure at Dealstruck was spent making sure that people kept working and that DLI kept paying them until we finished transitioning the portfolio to a new servicer.

Aside from the obvious draw of a paycheck, one of the main attractions of showing up every day was the impromptu performances of our salesman-turned-insult comic, Alex (though if you ask him, he'd say he was insult comic-turned-salesman). I was introduced to Alex by my father, Neil, who had made a habit of delivering lectures on entrepreneurship to inmates at various prisons in and around San Diego County—talk about a captive audience! (Cue cheesy joke music.) Alex heard my dad speak a couple months before his release from an eighteen-month sentence at a local military prison for cavorting with a female officer who, inconveniently, also happened to be his Captain's daughter. I needed entry-level salespeople and my dad couldn't stop telling me about Alex's "gift of gab." So, I gave him a shot.

Though I've always thought myself a very regular guy, the truth is, as an Ivy League grad and a card-carrying member of the Lucky

Sperm Club, I'd spent most of my adult life around people with similar credentials. My colleagues on Wall Street and at Ampush went to fancy schools, held fancy jobs, and could afford fancy things. Dealstruck was my first exposure to the working class beyond a slice of a pie chart in a Census Bureau report. I didn't think I harbored any biases until I caught myself one day surprised by my own surprise at how talented some of my lowest paid workers were. For not much more than minimum wage, I had employees with checkered personal and professional histories working harder, working smarter, and simply outperforming clean-cut, college-educated guys with resumes.

A couple months into the wind-down, I did a small consulting project for a well-funded Bay Area competitor that was struggling to scale its internal sales team. They'd hired, at near six-figure salaries, a team of telesales agents and business development reps that were far under-performing what our team at Dealstruck had done—and my team had done it for one-third the cost (a *big* difference even adjusted for cost-of-living). Their team, as constructed, was apparently the product of an internal debate as to whether a bunch of *"hardcore, uneducated, tatted up grinders"* would hurt the company's otherwise techie-bourgeois culture. It's possible they might have. But a bunch of "brilliant jerks" might, too. If you enter the relationship *assuming* there will be a problem, you're likely to be right.[58]

I'd like to think Dealstruck was not the first time this group had been given an honest chance to be part of a team, to be recognized for their contributions, to be treated like "skilled" labor, but the firmness with which they gripped their opportunity made me think it was. I'm not suggesting there weren't bad apples, or that there wasn't turnover. Nor am I suggesting these team members could fix broken code, build financial models, or review legal documents. What I am saying is that implicit bias is far more rampant and more subtly pernicious than we're aware.

---

58   A variant of Henry Ford's original quote, "Whether you think you can, or you think you can't—you're right."

Under the proper conditions, your "unskilled" labor can be some of your most valuable.

While we're on the topic of labor, I still had my share of people problems during the wind-down phase.

If there was one person who should have been ecstatic about the situation, it was our Special Assets Manager,[59] Rob. When a finance company goes under, there is a natural increase in portfolio deterioration as some borrowers who become aware of their lender's financial straits stop paying on the assumption a discount or settlement will be forthcoming. So, when I broke the news it was Game Over, everyone was downright sullen except for Rob—he was the umbrella salesman in a rainstorm, and he knew it.

Having already received a couple raises since joining Dealstruck, Rob was so excited about his retention package that he came into my office minutes after the final layoff to shake my hand and to assure me he would be "here through the end." For a guy who was hired away from a $65k per year job at Chase Bank less than one year ago, Rob's new annual salary was $101k and he was guaranteed a minimum of three months' severance. Which is why I found it bizarre when he informed me—just before New Year's Eve 2016—he'd be leaving for another job.

After a bit of arm-wringing, I'd convinced Rob to stay—he told me directly he would turn the other offer down. However, in the weeks after the holidays, his behavior changed. He started dictating his hours, working from home, and asking for more money. When it came to light he had actually taken the other job and was trying to double-dip, I fired him and, on his way out, deducted from his PTO bank all the hours he'd skipped without approval.

A few weeks later, I received notice from the California Labor Commission that Rob had filed a claim for his PTO hours. At our mediation hearing, he admitted that he was working two jobs—violating the terms of his employment with Dealstruck—and

---

59 "Special assets" is industry jargon for loans that have progressed beyond an early stage of delinquency and that require more serious attention and action.

that he hadn't been coming into the office as required during normal business hours. He had no case, so when I offered a $1k settlement on a $4k claim to spare me future headache, my HR Manager scowled and kicked me under the table. Needless to say, Rob rejected the offer. Two months later, the week before we shut down for good, I received a letter from the Labor Commission informing me Rob had changed his mind—he'd settle for one thousand dollars. That letter went straight to the shredder.

If Rob had simply hung around for sixty days, he would have taken home nearly $30k in severance and accrued PTO, and, in all likelihood, still gotten the same job. But he couldn't control his impulses.

It turns out the inability to delay gratification has serious long-term consequences. In a famous study—The Stanford Marshmallow Experiment[60]—children were placed in a room with a table, on top of which sat a plate with one marshmallow. The experimenter explained to each child they could eat the marshmallow anytime they pleased, but if they waited only fifteen minutes, they would be rewarded with two of the sweet treats. One-third of the participants managed to hold out. When the researchers revisited the participants at various intervals over the next fifty years, they found that the group of children who were able to delay gratification had higher SAT scores, lower levels of substance abuse, lower risk for obesity, better social skills as reported by their parents, better responses to stress, and generally better scores on a range of other life measures.[61]

Convincing people to override their impulses is a big part of CEO-ing. Even though you're doing it because it's in your company's best interest, it's most likely in theirs, too.

---

60   Walter Mischel, Ebbe Ebbensen, and Antonette Raskoff Zeiss, "Cognitive and Attentional Mechanisms in Delay Gratification," *Journal of Personality and Social Psychology* 21, no. 2 (1972): 204-218.

61   Synopsis and links to follow-up studies can be found at http://jamesclear.com/delayed-gratification.

The same week that Rob became a problem child, my co-founder also became one. It was easy enough for the remaining team to pick up Rob's caseload, but Russell, being the only engineer left on staff, was in a more privileged position. On a day-to-day basis, there wasn't much technology aid needed, so I looked the other way when Russell decided to move to San Francisco while still on the payroll. As long as he stayed responsive and kept Dealstruck his top priority, I didn't much care what he did with the rest of his time, nor where he did it from.

But he didn't stay responsive.

When DLI—who was paying our salaries—had an email request ignored for a week, they became irate. Their bulldog general counsel drove down from LA, marched into our office, and, in a conference room with paper-thin walls, yelled, "No one is fucking working. We're not paying shit!" He was wrong about us. Everyone there was working hard. But he was right about Russell.

So, we made a deal. DLI would pay everyone's severance on the condition that Russell forewent his.

It was a fair trade. Though he'd been getting paid full-time for a few short hours of work each week, Russell failed to uphold his end of the bargain. I called him to break the news—his $15k severance wouldn't be paid. He was irate.

"I don't owe DLI shit. I'm a market of one. They want me to work? Fucking pay me."

For a computer scientist, Russell had developed a pretty sound understanding of the economics of supply-and-demand. But this wasn't about math, this was about decency, about finishing with dignity, about doing the right thing. He didn't agree. Until he was assured he would be paid his severance, he told me, "I'm not lifting a finger."

Unable to compel him and unwilling to risk everyone else's safety net by revisiting the subject with an already short-tempered DLI, I bit the bullet. The next morning, I sent Russell a text message. His severance was reinstated. What I didn't tell him was that I'd be paying it personally.

Every CEO has people problems. That's as certain as the sun rising or waves breaking or snow melting. But I figured once the company stopped operating in normal course, those problems would stop, too. After all, didn't anyone consider how difficult this situation was for *me*? Wouldn't they play nice until we finished the transition for *my* sake? Couldn't they be sensitive to the problems *I* had?

As my sister and I have grown up, I've often noticed a juvenile quality resurface uncontrollably in both of us whenever we find ourselves reunited for a holiday weekend at our mom's house—staying in the same rooms, eating at the same table, and laughing at the same jokes as we did when we were kids. Regardless of our own professional circumstances or our own familial development, we can't shake the fact that we will always be our parents' children and, in all likelihood, we will always act that way, too. As my folks are apt to say, "Parenting never stops." The same can be said of running a company. So long as you have a team—big or small, operating or liquidating, blue-collar or white—CEO-ing never stops.

In the process of winding down, you will come to a point where there simply isn't much left to do. It will feel a bit like being ahead by thirty points in the fourth quarter of a basketball game—both sides know the outcome is certain and would rather hit the showers early, but you still have to run out the clock.

This is where we found ourselves in late February 2017 when it was decided that on March 31st, Dealstruck would be no more.

My last thirty days were filled with all of the obvious emotions—disappointment, anger, regret, and nostalgia, but some not-so-obvious feelings surfaced, too.

Jealousy was one of them.

From the moment we announced our layoff and impending shutdown, competitors and recruiters alike had descended on our best talent to offer them jobs or to help land them their next ones. Having just terminated fifty people and having set an expiration date for the remaining few, watching my team members parlay their Dealstruck experience into exciting new endeavors should have filled me with pride and relief—pride that their time at Dealstruck was not in vain, and relief that their exit from Dealstruck hadn't caused pain (at least not financially). Instead, I felt envy. That their phone was ringing and not mine. That their skills were in demand and mine weren't. That they were ready for next and I wasn't.

One of the fundamental tenets of logic is the Law of Identity.[62] We commoners know it more colloquially as an "entity is the sum of its parts." Dealstruck, though, seemed to honor its inverse. At once, the whole was a failure, but its parts were a success. My envy arose because I identified as the former.

This is an affliction common to most founders and CEOs—the mistaken assumption that because an idea was borne from our mind and guided by our hand, we are something more than one of its component pieces. It's true we are a *central* piece, a *salient* piece, and an *influential* piece. But we are only *one* piece. Believing this won't absolve us from being accountable to our stakeholders; it won't exempt us from being tarnished with failure's brush; it won't pardon us from being aware of our imperfect leadership. What it will do is allow us to consider the possibility that our companies can fail completely without us being complete failures.

Just because your company went broke, you are not broken. Unless you choose to be, that is.

It was this realization that engendered a second, unexpected emotion in my waning days at Dealstruck, an emotion that would triumph over envy—optimism.

Over the past fifteen years, the bulk of my therapy dollars have been spent trying to internalize the notion that we are the source of our experience of the world. We can't control everything that happens around us or that happens to us, but we can control how we interpret these events. Every single moment of every single day we are an active participant in the construction of our own reality. Our circumstances may not always be a choice, but how we feel about

---

62   The Law of Identify is the first of Aristotle's three laws of thought. It posits that A is A, or that "everything is the same as itself."

them, and how we react to them, is. That the outside universe has no more meaning than that which we *choose* to ascribe to it is an empowering awareness. It means we decide if a company collapse is an abject failure or an opportunity to learn; we decide if an employee's next act is an attack on our competence or a reflection of it; we decide if five years, thirty million dollars, an empty office, and a broken lease is wasted time or time we won't let be a waste.

This hit home for me when my most philosophical employee became my most virulent ex-employee. Angered over receiving the same severance package as others despite his longer tenure, he called to tell me that I'd mismanaged the company, mismanaged the wind-down, lied to him overtly, exploited his labor, and that my inability to find him an extra five grand left him *no choice* but to think back on Dealstruck and on me with hostility and anger.

I didn't agree with his assessment, but I wasn't interested in arguing.

"I'm sorry you feel that way," I said. "I know the outcome here has been difficult, and I feel terribly for how things ended. I really hope you'll take something away from Dealstruck other than resentment. But it's up to you."

One of my favorite sayings is, "Experience is what you get when you don't get what you want." By the last week of Dealstruck, I could no more undo the bad that had transpired than I could re-create the good.

All I was left with was an experience and a choice.

Dealstruck had been a remarkable journey. As I hugged my remaining teammates one final time, I was overcome with gratitude for the past, acceptance of the present, and hope for the future.

I zipped up my backpack, left my office keys on the counter, and switched out the lights.

After three years building up, one year turning around, and six months winding down, I was done.

next

AFTER THE DUST SETTLED, the question most commonly posed to me by witnesses of the Dealstruck debacle was, "Would you do it again?" When I told people my next act would involve a nine, a five, a paycheck and a boss, they mostly called bullshit—the prevailing wisdom being that entrepreneurship chooses you rather than you choosing it. They said that I'd never be happy in a normal job, that I wouldn't be able to report to a manager, and that the leisurely pace of corporate life would drive me insane. If there's one thing people like more than a victory, it's a comeback victory. But rooting for the underdog is easy when you're not the dog.

Building a startup had taken a serious toll. I was intellectually exhausted, physically drained, and emotionally bankrupt. Successful entrepreneurs don't feel all that differently, but a few million dollars affords them time to nurse the resultant wounds. For the rest of us, leaving empty-handed makes the question of "Next" a more urgent one. As painful as a significant loss may be, the most dangerous part of walking away holding nothing is the temptation to grab anything—a state referred to as "being on the rebound."

Those of us who have ever had something we care dearly about slip through our grasp—which is probably all of us—know firsthand the irresistible compulsion to recapture any shred of whatever it is we just lost. In our personal lives, research on "the rebound" suggests that when we are victims of a breakup—especially after a long-term, committed relationship—we are significantly more likely to engage in sex for motives of revenge, coping, and self-affirmation. Furthermore, it's been demonstrated that people who do this suffer "greater difficulty transitioning to a stable new partnership."[63] Rebound sex may seem off-topic, but given the frequency with which I've heard entrepreneurs refer to their startups as a spouse or significant other, the comparison seems apropos.

What all this means for your professional life is that the moment after you've been dumped, fired, laid off, or rejected—and closing a company is *all* of these things—you are pretty damn likely to go do exactly the thing you shouldn't do if you want to move on healthily. Jumping into Next immediately after a failure is as good a recipe for finding professional edification as sleeping with a random person walking down the block is for finding true love.

If I wasn't yet in a position to answer whether I *would* start another company, I was in a position to consider how I would operate *if* I did. It's one thing—as I've done in this book—to document lessons learned from a sequence of stressful startup scenarios with the benefit of hindsight and from the comfort of my living room sofa. It's quite another to apply those lessons when similar situations inevitably surface in the heat of subsequent battle.

There is a psychological phenomenon known as "anchoring" in which "people's answers to a question are influenced by thinking about an arbitrary value as a possible answer . . . ."[64] In one famous experiment, participants were asked to predict the percentage of African countries in the United Nations after a "wheel of fortune"

63   Lindsay L. Barber and M. Lynne Cooper, "Rebound Sex: Sexual Motives and Behaviors Following a Relationship Breakup," *Archives of Sexual Behavior* 43, no. 2 (December 2013): 251–265.

64   Timothy D. Wilson, Christopher E. Houston, and Kathryn M. Etling, "A New Look at Anchoring Effects: Basic Anchoring and Its Antecedents," *Journal of Experimental Psychology* 125, no. 4 (1996): 387–402.

was spun in their presence to provide a random initial estimate (the "anchor"). Those who landed on higher numbers guessed percentages significantly higher than those who got lower numbers, despite the anchor having no relation to the quantity in question.

While it may not be a shock to learn that our behavior can be manipulated subconsciously, what might be more surprising is that these techniques—of which anchoring is one—can be equally effective in influencing our actions when we are conscious of their existence. Researchers at the University of Virginia asked participants to estimate the number of physicians in the local phone book. The control group did not receive an anchor, the experimental group did (on the high side). Only this time, before guessing, members of the experimental group were given a definition of anchoring bias, an example of its "contaminating effect," and an explicit warning:

> *When you answer the questions on the following pages,*
> *please be careful not to have this contamination effect happen*
> *to you. We would like the most accurate estimates that you can*
> *come up with.*

As you might suspect by now, the control group estimated 219 physicians, whereas the experimental group estimated an amount nearly three times larger. This result led researchers to conclude that anchoring effects still existed "when people were blatantly provided with anchor values and explicitly told not to use these values when answering subsequent questions."

It turns out that being aware of faults in our thought patterns or biases in our methods of decision-making doesn't exempt us from falling prey to these so-called cognitive blind spots when it comes time to think and decide.

This is particularly concerning since, although I've shared technical takeaways from my experience as a startup CEO—hiring, firing, fundraising, and the like—the most important lessons are psychological in nature. The reality of business, including the startup variety, is that a working knowledge of its functional aspects is within reach of anyone reading at a high-school level and possessing a curious mind. Building financial models, defining product features, setting compensation schemes, and negotiating term sheets will not be your biggest challenges. Submerging your ego, broadening your perspective, balancing your life, comforting your colleagues, taming your anxieties, and maintaining the courage of your convictions will be.

As I come to the end of my tale, what concerns me most is not whether next time will be different, but whether next time *I* will be different. Though I'd like to think a two-hundred-page dissertation on the crux of my failing will be enough to guarantee I won't repeat the same mistakes, the evidence suggests that awareness alone may not be enough to prevent me from being fooled twice.

But enough about me. Let's talk about you.

If you've made it to this point, you've taken a journey into the business and personal life of a guy who has done a few things right, but many more things wrong. As the perpetrator of these mistakes, not even I'm immune from relapse. Which begs the question: How can you, as an observer, transform my missteps into preparations, strategies, and defense mechanisms of your own?

There is a rich body of research evidence proving that, as far as learning business skills, "success depends on a combination of intellectual comprehension and hands-on experience"[65]—a process known as experiential learning. This type of learning consists of four steps: (a) concrete experience; (b) reflective observation; (c) abstract conceptualization; and (d) active experimentation. What I've done in the preceding pages is share with you my experience, reflect on it, and distill from it concrete suggestions for how to navigate common startup snafus.

But where my analysis ends is where yours begins. As you hold up your experiences against the information gleaned from this book, hopefully, you will be able to integrate the two into a set of behaviors that helps you become a more effective entrepreneur, leader, or

---

65   Claus Benkert and Nick van Dam, "Experiential Learning: What's Missing in Most Change Programs," *McKinsey Quarterly* (August 2015).

manager than you'd be otherwise. Maybe you'll adopt all of my pre-scriptions, maybe only some, maybe none. But if you think about them critically in light of your own journey—assess their applicability, build them up, or break them down entirely—you'll have used them well.

The most important part of consolidating information and experience into learning, in order to turn it into lasting change and measurable growth, is to experiment.

And, in this, we are together.

Before writing this epilogue, I spent a few weeks abroad, com-pletely removed from the story I'd immersed myself in telling for eight months (and living for years before that). Professional writers told me separating myself from my text would be good; that when I returned to finalize my work, the perspective created by time and distance would allow me to sharpen my storyline, energize my expe-riences, and tighten my takeaways.

Unfortunately, nothing of the sort happened.

Rather than returning better able to enliven my story, I returned completely detached from it. As I reread chapter after chapter, I could hardly believe the subject, the writer, and the reader were the same person. When I tried to revisit my ordeal with an emotional intensity that remotely rivaled what I felt while living through it and writing about it, I couldn't come close.

For months I'd been waiting for this dramatic moment, but when it finally arrived, it was no more than a few seconds of wistfulness. The only true pain I felt was the dull ache of indifference that signi-fies moving on.

The fact that reminiscing on Dealstruck no longer triggered any emotional angst is—according to most mental health experts—an indication of psychological well-being. It's also a sign that closure is nigh, that my time to experiment has come—and that Next is now, appropriately enough, right around the corner.

So, will I do it again? I hope so. Will I do it differently? Yes.

acknowledgments

I **WOULD HAVE PREFERRED** not to have been able to write this book. This story came at a significant cost to my investors, my lenders, my vendors, and my employees; people who believed in my vision and my leadership and who, in ways big and small, suffered for doing so. As you by now know, we had our disagreements along the way, but I'm keenly aware that there would have been no Dealstruck without them and I'm forever grateful for the opportunity they afforded me to pursue a dream. Though a few lines of gratitude won't replace their lost money, time, or energy, I hope they will combine with the complete and candid recount in the preceding pages to be some form of consolation.

Entrepreneurship is a business that you only learn fully the "hard way," but I was blessed to be surrounded by intelligent, generous, and committed professionals who tried to make my road easier. Chief among these was Zalman, who cared for me like his son and trained me like his protégé, and who stood by me to the bitter end. Noel, too, even in moments of frustration, disappointment, and anger—of which there were plenty—always spoke with a subtext of optimism, encouragement, and support. Notwithstanding the mild lump that formed in my throat whenever Brendan's number lit up my phone screen, he also treated my team and me with fairness and respect until the door on Dealstruck closed one final time.

That the people I'm most thankful to were some of the people with whom I had the most intense conflicts speaks to the inherent messiness of creating something from nothing. I'm certain that the uncomfortable deliberations, disagreements, and disputes we had were of the precise nature required for any startup to realize its small probability of success. Though surrounding myself with people willing to express their perspectives, challenge my decision-making, and engage constructively in conflict was insufficient to generate a win, doing so was still necessary for me to have ever had a chance.

If the entrepreneur spends most of his (or her) conscious moments worried about his business, his family and friends spend an equal amount of time worrying about him. Were it not for the daily expressions of unconditional love I received outside of the office, the Dealstruck story would have ended much sooner. That I fought to the end—leaving no stone unturned in my search for a solution—was due more to the resilience of my loved ones, than to my own. Though their names did not appear on the cap table, they were as heavily invested in Dealstruck, and in me, as any who did. The list of people who deserve explicit acknowledgment is too long to print in full, but a few deserve special mention: my sister calling me each morning to express unwavering belief, my mom preparing a comforting meal at the end of each week, my wife reminding me that everything—no matter what—would be okay.

One name conspicuously missing from the prior paragraphs is my father, Neil. There is no one for whom these two hundred pages and the five years they encapsulate are more painful. As an advisor, investor, lender, and early Board member, the fact of our biological linkage largely became an afterthought for both of us during the Dealstruck saga. It had to be. I remember many Sunday night dinners overrun by arguments and misery about the latest Dealstruck dealings, after which my father would lean back in resignation and sigh, "I just want my son back." Well, here I am. That our relationship not only survived Dealstruck, but has thrived in its aftermath is a manifestation of love far exceeding that which any son could expect from his father.

The ability to share my story in a remotely coherent way is thanks to the dedication of my editor, Jennifer Redmond, my publishing manager, Karla Olson, and my designer, Charles McStravick. Each of them devoted far more to this book than rational self-interest would dictate. They treated an amateur, first-time author like an established veteran, and brought my words to life with an emotional intensity rivaled only by the experiences they describe.

As with any "thank you" speech, I'm sure there are people I'm forgetting to mention, but I'd rather stop now than get played off stage. My hope is that those whom I may have overlooked in these acknowledgments know who they are and that my expressions of gratitude outside the four corners of this book have impressed upon them the valuable role they played in my journey.

Lastly, to my reader, thank you. Words on paper can do no good to the world if they remain unread. I hope you found investing in my story to be useful and I look forward to one day reading your tale of the grand adventures that surely await you.

about
the author

ETHAN SENTURIA IS AN ENTREPRENEUR, advisor, author, and investor. He most recently served as co-founder and CEO of Dealstruck, an online business lending platform, the story of which inspired his first book, Unwound: Real-time Reflections of a Stumbling Entrepreneur. At Dealstruck, Senturia raised over $150m of institutional debt and equity, and led a seventy person team on its mission to provide fair and transparent financial products to growing small businesses. Prior to Dealstruck, Ethan was on the founding team of Ampush, a successful performance marketing company, where he led customer acquisition as Vice President of Online Media. He started his career as a credit research analyst on Wall Street after graduating Summa Cum Laude from the Wharton School of Business